PCs made easy

made easy

STAGE 7

A PRACTICAL COURSE

PCs made easy

easy

STAGE 7

A PRACTICAL COURSE

PUBLISHED BY THE READER'S DIGEST ASSOCIATION LIMITED
LONDON   NEW YORK   SYDNEY   MONTREAL

PCS MADE EASY
A PRACTICAL COURSE – STAGE 7

Published by the Reader's Digest Association Limited, 2002

The Reader's Digest Association Limited
11 Westferry Circus, Canary Wharf, London E14 4HE
www.readersdigest.co.uk

We are committed to both the quality of our products and the service we
provide to our customers, so please feel free to contact us on 08705 113366,
or via our Web site at www.readersdigest.co.uk
If you have any comments or suggestions about the content
of this book, e-mail us at:
gbeditorial@readersdigest.co.uk

®Reader's Digest, The Reader's Digest and the Pegasus
logo are registered trademarks of The Reader's Digest
Association Inc, of Pleasantville, New York, USA

For Reader's Digest
Series Editor: Christine Noble
Assistant Editor: Caroline Boucher
Art Editor: Julie Bennett

Reader's Digest General Books
Editorial Director: Cortina Butler
Art Director: Nick Clark

PCs made easy was created and produced for
The Reader's Digest Association Limited by De Agostini UK Ltd,
from material originally published as the Partwork
Computer Success Plus.

Printing and binding: Printer Industria Gráfica S.A., Barcelona

ISBN 0 276 42639 8

CONTENTS

Windows

The Stand-by command

Switching off your computer means you have to wait for it to start up each time you use it. But you can safely leave it on for long periods – and save time and energy – by using power-management options.

In an environmentally conscious world, the way you set up your computer can play its part in minimizing unnecessary energy consumption. We've already shown how to use Windows' screen saver options to reduce power usage (see Stage 6, pages 12-13), but you can cut down usage even further by specifying an idle time – after which the computer will switch the monitor into a low-power sleep mode. This will minimize the power consumed by the monitor when you are not using the PC.

However, even though a dormant monitor consumes a fraction of the power it does when in use, the computer itself is still fully operational and using power at the same rate as if you were still typing.

NOTEBOOK POWER

Windows provides extra options for notebooks that allow you to squeeze the maximum life out of the battery. For example, many notebooks have an extra tab called Hibernate in the Power Management Properties window. This lets you switch on a special feature that can save time and battery power. If you tick the Enable hibernate support box (below), your notebook will go into a very deep sleep. Every time you close the lid, Windows copies data from memory to the hard disk and shuts down automatically.

When your computer comes out of hibernation, Windows restarts and copies the data back into memory – so you're exactly where you left off without having to start up and reopen documents or programs.

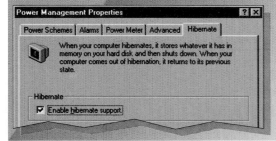

```
Power Management Properties                    ? X
Power Schemes | Alarms | Power Meter | Advanced | Hibernate |

     When your computer hibernates, it stores whatever it has in
     memory on your hard disk and then shuts down. When your
     computer comes out of hibernation, it returns to its previous
     state.

Hibernate
  ☑ Enable hibernate support.
```

● The Stand-by mode

Windows' special Stand-by mode drastically reduces the amount of power used by the computer itself. Its processor chip slows right down when you don't need it. With the screen saver options, the computer automatically keeps track of how long it was since you last pressed a key or moved the mouse before it switches the monitor into low-power mode. By contrast, to switch the computer into Stand-by mode, you must select a special option from the Shut Down Windows dialog box.

● Instant action

Once you have selected the Stand-by option, the screen blanks out and the hard disk stops spinning. To all intents and purposes, the PC appears to be switched off. But as soon as it detects input, such as movement of the mouse, the computer will burst back into life, exactly at the point you left it earlier.

If you put your computer on stand-by when it's not being used, you will save on both power consumption and time. Just hit a key or move the mouse and the PC will 'wake up' much more quickly than from a cold start.

WINDOWS ME

Windows Me closely follows the format of Windows 98, at least for the purposes of the average user. Therefore, unless indicated otherwise, all the exercises in *PCs made easy* work on both operating systems, with only minor differences in screen layout.

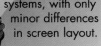

Power-saving options for Windows

Using the Stand-by command instead of Shut Down saves power and leaves your PC in a state where it can get back into action more quickly than when starting up from cold.

1 To see how the Stand-by command works, first select Shut Down from the Start menu.

2 In the dialog box, select Stand by and then press the OK button. After a moment, the screen goes blank. Inside the PC, the hard disk has also stopped spinning and the processor chip is operating at a lower **clock speed**.

WHAT IT MEANS

CLOCK SPEED

This is the rate at which a chip processes data. For example, when you're using a 800MHz computer, it's making 800 million data operations every single second.

3 However, the computer isn't totally dormant – it's still waiting for any input from you. Move the mouse a little and the PC starts up, with the screen exactly as you left it.

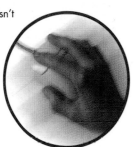

4 Windows keeps all information in the computer's memory intact, so any documents you were working on are exactly the same. However, any loss of power to the PC will cause all unsaved changes to your documents to be lost, so it's safest to save or close any documents you are working on before switching to Stand-by mode.

1 If you don't want to use Stand-by mode, but do want to save power, you can still fine-tune the settings for Windows' power management. Bring up the Control Panel by clicking on Settings in the Start menu and double-click on the Power Management icon.

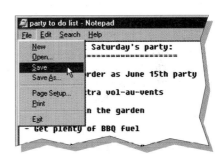

WATCH OUT

A computer that is left in Stand-by mode can look as if it is switched off. If you forget you have left it in that mode and then try to switch it on, you can inadvertently lose your data that is still in the memory. Always move the mouse or press a keyboard button first to check if the computer is just 'asleep'.

2 Under the Power Schemes tab, you can change the settings that control how long a period of inactivity lasts before Windows shuts down the monitor and the hard disk. On this PC the monitor switches off after 15 minutes of no mouse or keyboard input, but the hard disk never switches off.

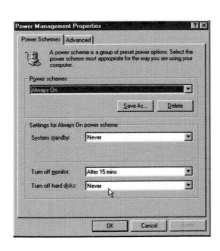

3 You can experiment with different settings. Bear in mind that each time the monitor turns back on and the hard disk spins back up to full speed, you are kept waiting. Short settings can prove frustrating, so try to find the right balance between environmental friendliness and inconvenience.

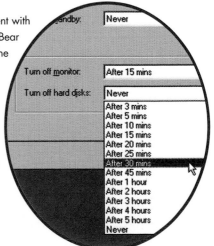

Windows security

You don't have to be paranoid to want a bit of privacy and security on your PC. Windows can supply some of the protection you need against unauthorized use of your PC or examination of your confidential files.

The main security measure built into Windows is the password protection system for its screen savers.

We show you how to set up this feature on page 12 but, in truth, it's not the most secure system and can be bypassed by a determined interloper.

The basic idea is a good one: once the screen saver is activated, you have to type in a password to turn it off and return to the Desktop. In theory, if you don't know the password you can't use the PC. The only problem is that anyone who doesn't know the password can simply restart the PC and load Windows again from scratch (see Microsoft and security box, opposite). Any files and programs that were previously open won't be immediately visible – but if the intruder knows where they are, or uses the Documents menu, where the most recently used files can be accessed, they can simply be opened up again.

● User profiles

Windows has another form of in-built security in the form of the User Profiles option (see Stage 6, pages 8-9). You can set up a separate 'user account' for everybody who uses your PC. Each person has a separate user name and password which must be entered when the PC starts up. When their password is typed in, they are presented with a Desktop and file system customized to their own preferences.

Again, this isn't fail-safe security. Although someone would need to know your password in order to view or alter your user settings, anyone can access any normal file on the PC simply by clicking the Cancel button when the Password window appears. Windows will then start up. Clearly, additional measures need to be taken if you want to make it really difficult for unauthorized users to get into your PC.

Security is just as important for the home computer user as it is for commercial organizations. Selecting the right security package means you can choose how accessible, or not, you want your PC to be.

● Extra security measures

If none of these standard Windows security measures is foolproof, what can be done by the ordinary Windows user who wants to protect his or her computer data?

As you might expect with such an obvious gap in the market, a number of shareware and third-party programs claim to offer absolute security options for your PC. Many of these packages are aimed directly at the corporate user and are, therefore, on the expensive side. However, there are several packages targeted specifically at the home user and we look at the more popular of these on page 13.

Many of these add-ons are reasonably priced and work extremely well, not just by adding an unbreakable password system to your computer but also with more subtle security. For example, you might wish to protect certain files or folders, or perhaps restrict access to certain programs.

SIMPLE SECURITY

As there are ways around Windows' screen saver password, don't forget that some programs let you password protect your documents. If you have a family finances spreadsheet in Excel, for example, you can add a password when you save it, to keep it out of sight of children who may share your PC (see Stage 2, page 62).

SECURITY

● Protecting children

A lot of people want security protection, largely to stop their children from playing around with the Desktop – and any other settings they may happen to access. Many of the home security packages aim to overcome this problem by disabling the important Desktop customization options and keeping a permanent back-up of your preferred settings.

Not everyone wants to turn their PC into an impenetrable fortress, but most people do want a bit of privacy. Also, if you have children it is actually in their interests to ensure that your computer has some security measures. After all, it's one thing for your kids to go rooting through the family accounts, but quite another thing if they randomly surf the Internet and come across sites which you don't feel are suitable. Rather than using one of the child-minding programs (see Stage 4, pages 138-141), which can sometimes be rather limited, it's much easier to limit your child's online excursions by simply password-protecting your Web browser. By using this feature you can ensure that they only ever explore the Internet when you are around, thus enabling you to make the decisions about what they should be viewing.

MICROSOFT AND SECURITY

It might seem a little careless to have a standard password system that can be bypassed simply by restarting the PC, but computer security is a notoriously difficult area. Microsoft have certainly struggled to get it right. In the early 1990s the company had a lot of trouble convincing the US military that Windows NT was safe enough for them to use. The US Army was very concerned about a number of apparent loopholes and refused to use the standard version of the software for even the simplest of tasks.

Password alternatives

Other options available range from random questions and facial selections to retinal scans.

ENSURING THAT ONLY the right people access sensitive systems is difficult. A balance has to be struck between having security systems that are secure, but are also easy to operate.

Password-based security is certainly simple to operate, which is its strength – but also its weakness. For instance, some of the basic passwords can be worked out simply by exhaustive repetition of variations until you strike lucky. Also, passwords are set up to be easy to remember, but despite this, they are frequently forgotten. For this reason, people may write down their passwords and this makes the whole system much more vulnerable. The first thing that someone who is trying to break into a password-protected system does is to look for some scrap of paper nearby or among a person's possessions.

Alternatives have been invented that are better at ensuring that only accredited people can gain access to computer systems. One method involves users providing a set of facts about such things as their name, address, a memorable event or place. When they access the system they are asked one or more randomly picked questions about this information. This means that no one single piece of information can gain access to the system.

Another security method involves visual information. The log-on screen may show a collection of famous faces, for example. Access is gained by selecting the right set of faces. There is nothing to write down and as, according to research, our visual memory for faces is excellent, this method is very easy to operate and very secure. An extension to this method involves choosing a set of faces in the right sequence.

If you are absolutely determined to have no security doubts whatsoever and need to ensure that only an authorized person has access to your PC, then a fingerprint-type method could be an option. This does not use the fingers but the back of the eye. It is based on the fact that the pattern of blood vessels in a person's retina is unique. A camera takes a retinal scan of a person wanting to use the system. This is compared to previous scans filed on the system. If there is a match, then access is allowed. If there is no match, then a security breach has been attempted and appropriate action can be taken.

The unique pattern of blood vessels found at the back of the retina of the human eye enables it to be used to identify a specific individual. This form of identification acts as a very effective security screening device, similar to the use of fingerprints.

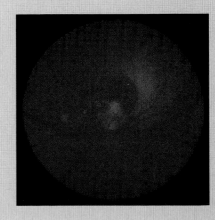

Setting up password protection

A screen saver password is not going to protect you against a determined intruder, but it's a very easy way to give yourself a degree of security.

1 The screen savers, and all options connected with them, are controlled from the Display Properties window. The easiest way to access this important window is to right-click anywhere on the empty Desktop and select Properties from the pop-up menu.

2 The screen savers have a section of the window all to themselves. Click the Screen Saver tab at the top to access it. Don't worry if your Display Properties tabs are different from those pictured here, as the number and types of tabs depend on your graphics card and other associated devices.

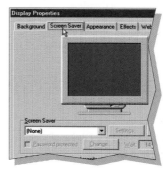

3 If you don't already have a screen saver set up, then you will have to enable one. There are a number of basic screen savers included with Windows. To choose whichever screen saver you want, just click on the Screen Saver pull-down menu and select a name from the list.

4 By default, password protection will be turned off. To enable it, simply tick the Password protected box. To set the password, click the Change button.

5 A new window will pop up for you to type in your password. You must do so twice, to confirm the characters you have typed (the letters are represented by asterisks on screen). The password can be any length and any combination of letters and numbers (see Password characters box, left). Click OK when you have finished.

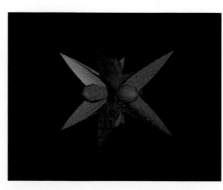

6 Once the password is fixed, you will want to set up the other screen saver options. Any cosmetic changes, which vary from screen saver to screen saver, are made by clicking the Settings button. The Wait box is the most important option, as this defines how soon the screen saver starts after the last time you used the mouse or keyboard.

7 In order to test how the password will work, click the Preview button. This will immediately start the screen saver you have selected. You usually turn off a screen saver by moving the mouse or pressing a keyboard button. If you try that now, however, you will be asked for your password.

8 In order to use the PC, you must enter the correct password; otherwise, your only alternative is to switch off the computer and start again.

Third-party security software

Bootlocker

www.bootlocker.com/bl
Eppler Software – $23.95 (approx £17.00)
BootLocker gives you tighter control than the Windows screen saver password protection. Once installed, an extra icon appears in the Windows System Tray. You can use this icon to put the PC into a state of instant suspended animation. Only by typing in the correct password is the PC brought back to life.

The program is designed to block the tricks that snoopers use to get past the standard Windows screen saver password (see opposite). For example, the [Ctrl]+[Alt]+[Del] key stroke is blocked and, even if the PC is restarted, BootLocker loads again. Of course, with any program that gives you such control over your PC, you need to make sure you never forget the password.

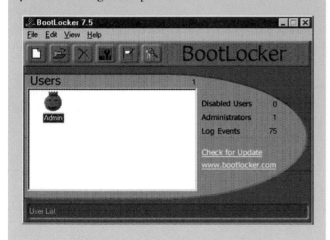

SecurDesk!

www.cursorarts.com/
CursorArts – $199.95 (approx £140.00)
Although SecurDesk! is a lot more expensive than most of its competitors, it is one of the more reliable and richly featured home security programs. It was originally intended for use in small- to medium-sized companies, where the need to secure computers and data was far more important. SecurDesk! comprises four main modules, each of which can be used separately or in combination. They are: Desktop, Task Manager, File Manager and Administration Manager. Each helps to control access to sensitive materials, as well as hiding confusing and irrelevant items from selected users.

The Desktop module deals with the everyday options, such as who can access the PC and what portions of the Desktop can be used by whom. It also allows you to customize the appearance of your Desktop with 'your own' toolbars and buttons, special function icons and automatically triggered programs. The Task Manager is used to store and maintain useful information and control system resources, while the File Manager monitors files, keeping tabs on when they have been modified, where backup copies exist, and ensuring that multiple copies of a file are properly catalogued. The Administration Manager controls overall security, with a huge range of passwords limiting access to specific programs, options, files, or the whole PC.

WINSelect

www.winselect.com/
Hyper Technologies – $49 (approx £35).
Hyper Technologies' WINSelect is actually a two-program set. WINSelect KIOSK (below, right) controls and disables any feature in any Windows program from the email option in a Web browser to the Minimize button on a folder. POLICY (below, left) controls security. It can also be used to disable startup and access, or to restrict users to specific folders, file types, printers or modems.

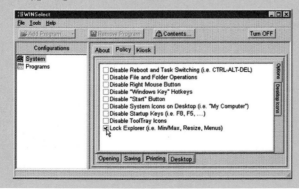
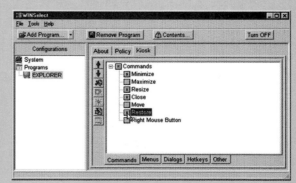

Task scheduling with Windows

With the Maintenance Wizard and Windows Task Scheduler, you can tell your computer to keep itself neat and tidy automatically – and even get it to do some of your work for you.

D espite the best of intentions to keep your PC's files in order, it's not always easy to make time for this essential task. While you might want to check your hard disk for problems and clean up unused files, there is usually more pressing 'real' work to do.

Fortunately, Windows comes with two very useful tools that can take care of these household chores for you. The Scheduled Tasks Wizard and the Maintenance Wizard can both be programmed to perform routine tasks whenever, and however often, you would like.

● **Other tasks**

You can also apply the same facilities to literally dozens of non-housekeeping tasks. You can tell Windows to start up any program at any time. If the program can automatically carry out certain actions when it starts up – checking for Internet email, for example – you can make sure that your computer is up and running and prepared for work even before you sit down in front of the screen.

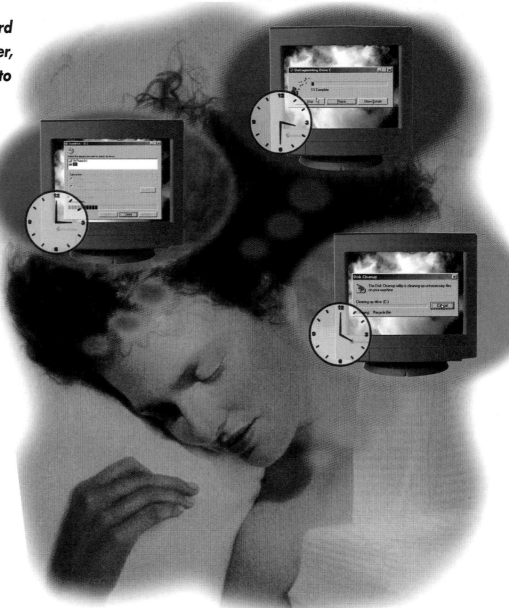

● **New tools**

The Maintenance Wizard is the all-purpose, central system tool. It rolls several utilities into one and you can specify which of those utilities you actually want it to run. It includes improved versions of ScanDisk, Disk Defragmenter and Disk Cleanup (see Stage 3, pages 8-11).

Make your computer look after itself by programming it to perform essential maintenance tasks when it's convenient for you.

You can specify when you want all these tools to run, and how often. This is important, because some of these routines – particularly those of Disk Defragmenter – can be time-consuming. Also, Disk Cleanup might try to dispose of files that, while not crucial, might be needed occasionally. So, you may not really want these routines running on your machine during the day while you're working or when you've turned your back on your computer for just a few minutes.

● Computer hibernation

Although Windows doesn't state it clearly, it does encourage you not to shut down your computer, particularly if you use it often and on a regular basis.

Instead of turning it off at night and switching on every morning, Windows would rather you used its advanced stand-by and hibernation features (see pages 8-9) to manage your sessions automatically. And there are several very good reasons for doing just that.

● Power stations

Depending on your hardware, you can tell your computer to shut down your monitor or hard disk automatically after a certain period of time, whether you've gone for lunch or finished for the day. Stand-by mode saves even more power. Once your computer has gone into hibernation, it takes a little while for it to awaken again, but it's much quicker than starting up from the beginning.

With Windows, the tasks you schedule automatically bring the PC out of hibernation. For example, the computer starts up late at night, runs the tasks you have scheduled for that time and then goes back to sleep again.

● Wake-up call

While the scheduling and hibernation features work well together for Windows maintenance and system tools, even more useful options are possible when you combine the scheduler with other programs on your PC. For example, you can set up your email program to log on to your Internet service provider, check your email mailbox and then log off again. We show you how to do this in the exercise on page 17.

Power management settings

Get your PC to work while you sleep or take a break.

LEAVING YOUR PC on overnight to run maintenance routines is a great idea but it potentially clashes with environmental concerns because you are using up hours of power just for a few minutes of computing.

To avoid this particular problem, you can set Windows' power management options so that power is only used for the time that the housekeeping and scheduled tasks are running. To avoid shutting down your PC, use the Control Panel's Power Management program instead. Choose the options that let your PC switch into either stand-by or Hibernate modes. For example, click the Advanced tab in the Power Management Properties window and tell

Windows to switch your PC into Stand-by mode when you press the PC On/Off switch. Windows can wake itself up from Stand-by mode to carry out the tasks you set up. Not all versions of Windows show the 'Wake the computer to run this task' option when using the scheduling tasks (see page 17), but as long as the PC is in Stand-by mode, it will wake up to perform the task at the specified time.

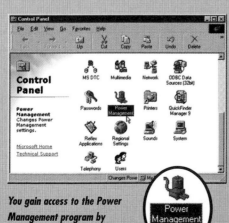

You gain access to the Power Management program by double-clicking on its icon in the Control Panel window (above).

Click on the Advanced tab on the Power Management Properties window and select Standby from the listbox under When I press the power button on my computer (right). This makes sure you leave your computer in Stand-by mode when you hit the power key, consuming less power but ready to leap into action when scheduled tasks are due.

Setting up the Maintenance Wizard

Here we show you how to use the Windows Maintenance Wizard to configure and schedule mundane, but necessary, system tasks.

1 From the Start menu, select the Maintenance Wizard command from the System Tools folder.

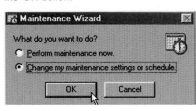

2 In the pop-up dialog box, select the Change my maintenance settings or schedule option and click on the OK button.

3 The Maintenance Wizard starts up. Select the Custom option and click the Next button.

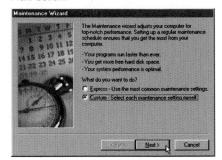

4 You can now choose when you want the maintenance tasks to run. We've gone for Nights. Click the Next button.

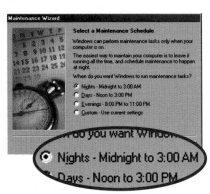

5 Windows asks you which programs you want to run. The ones they suggest often include useful utilities, so leave these settings as they are for the moment. Click the Next button.

6 The first screen covers defragmenting your hard disk. By default, the scheduler will do this weekly. This is too frequent for us, so click the Reschedule button and, in the dialog box that appears, change the Schedule Task setting to Monthly. Click the OK button.

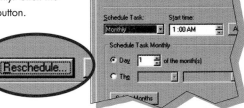

7 Windows asks about scanning your hard disk regularly. The weekly suggestion here is fine, but check what will happen on these scans by clicking the Settings button. Select all the hard disks in your computer, together with the Thorough and Automatically fix errors options, before clicking the OK button to continue.

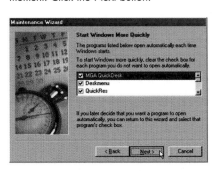

DISK CLEANUP SETTINGS

If you click the Settings button on the dialog box shown in Step 8, you can change the types of files that are automatically deleted by Windows.

8 The next screen allows you to specify which files Windows should automatically delete to free up disk space. For this exercise, simply click the Next button.

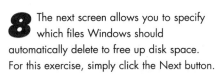
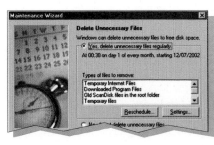

9 The Maintenance Wizard summarizes your choices, and confirms the dates and times when each task will run. Check each entry and, if necessary, use the Back button to return to previous screens to make any changes. Click the Finish button. Now, as long as your PC is switched on at the times shown, it will run these tasks automatically.

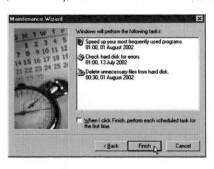

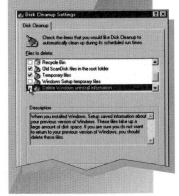

Automating email collection

By using the Scheduled Tasks Wizard with other Windows programs, you can get even more out of Windows. Here we show you how to collect email automatically in the early morning so that it's ready for you to read when you start up your PC.

1 From the Start menu, select the Scheduled Tasks item from the System Tools menu.

2 Double-click on the Add Scheduled Task item when the Scheduled Tasks folder opens.

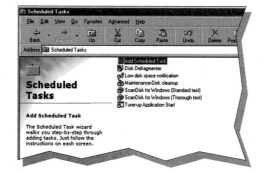

3 The Wizard takes you through the required steps: click the Next button on the first screen and again on the second. Select Outlook Express on this third screen (right) and then click on Next.

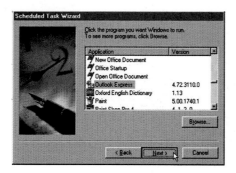

4 On the next screen, select the Daily option under the Perform this task section and then click on the Next button.

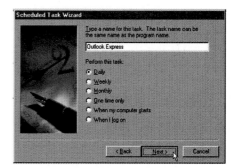

5 Enter the time and date when you want the email program to start. Choose a time as late as possible but within the off-peak period of your telephone company. Click on the Next button.

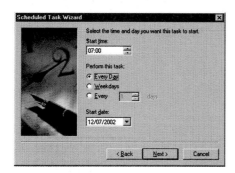

6 Tick the option labelled Open advanced properties for this task when I click Finish. Then, click on the Finish button.

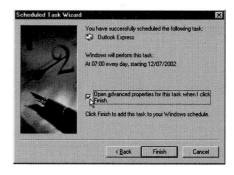

7 Click the Settings tab and tick the Stop the scheduled task after option. Insert 20 in the minutes box. Then, tick the Wake the computer to run this task option, then click the OK button (see Power management settings box, page 15).

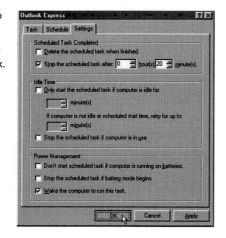

8 Now Outlook Express will start up at 7:00 every morning. It will automatically log on to your Internet account, check for email and log off. This particular email program normally checks every 30 minutes, so by getting the Task Scheduler to close the program after 20 minutes (see Step 7), it will check your email only once.

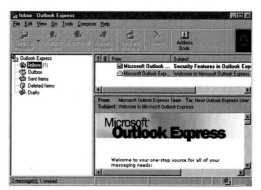

Windows Me games

If you want to take a short break from the stresses and strains of everyday Windows computing, have some fun with Windows Millennium Edition's suite of games.

When you feel like relaxing and forgetting about the drudgery of filing, formatting and backing up for a while, Windows provides its own distractions in the form of the Start menu's Games folder. Since its earliest days, Windows has always come with some simple, yet absorbing, games. Windows Millennium Edition adds even more variety. All of the Windows 98 games are still present, but Microsoft has included some extra games designed to appeal to solo and multi-player gamers alike.

● Fiendish games

Card games have always been popular, and Microsoft has added a new twist – Spider Solitaire. This is a fiendishly difficult version of the classic card game of patience. As usual, there are just a few simple rules, but even on the easiest of the three levels of difficulty you must concentrate to solve the puzzle. There is also Classic Solitaire – the version that was originally shipped with Windows 3.0 but was left out of the Windows 98 package. This is much truer to the original parlour version of the patience card game.

● Test your reflexes

If it's action and not relaxation you're after, there's also a fast-moving 3D Pinball game to keep you glued to the screen. Complete with Multimedia sound effects and great graphics, it includes all the typical extra-ball and flashing-light bonuses of a real arcade pinball machine. There are even keys that let you tilt the table – but don't do it too often or the pinball table freezes.

With the Internet considerably more popular now than when Windows 98 was planned, Microsoft has also included five Internet games. These are all versions of classic games – from backgammon to draughts. Unlike most online games, however, there is no awkward setup involved – you just start the game and connect to the Internet using your usual ISP. Once the connection is established, the game makes contact with the MSN Gaming Zone computer. After a short interval, during which the MSN computer locates a suitable opponent for you, the game can begin.

Windows Me has plenty of games on offer – Patience is just one of the many included as standard.

MORE ONLINE GAMES

The online games that Microsoft has chosen to include with Windows Me are just tasters of the full range of games available on the MSN Gaming Zone site. You can visit the site directly by typing the address www.zone.com into your Web browser and following the Free Signup links. Playing some of the games – such as those included with Windows Me – is free of charge, but other games might incur extra costs. You will see information on charges when you join.

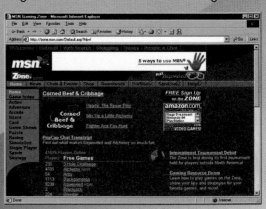

Play online with Windows Me

Play backgammon or checkers with someone on the other side of the world – Windows Millennium Edition comes with a selection of Internet games and some old favourites.

1 Click on the Start menu, then Programs and then Games. If you haven't used this folder for a while, you might find that Windows Me's personalized menus temporarily hide it from view. Pause the mouse for a few moments and the full menu listing will appear.

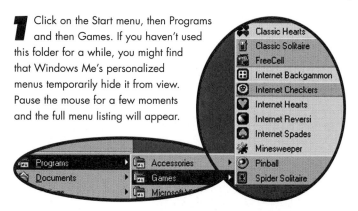

2 Try your hand – and your reflexes – at Pinball. Press and release the spacebar to send the ball into play and be ready with the [Z] key (for the left flipper) and the [/] key (for the right flipper) to keep the ball in play.

3 Spider Solitaire is a variant of patience. The aim is to remove cards from the face-up area. To do this you must create continuous, single-suit runs from Kings down to Aces. When no more moves are possible, you must deal another row of cards, which could spoil several good runs.

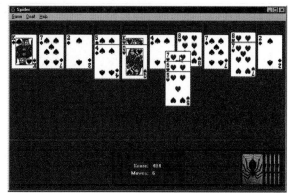

4 Spider Solitaire takes some time to master, and the default Difficulty setting of two suits can be tough going. To get used to the card movement rules try starting the game with the Easy One Suit option selected.

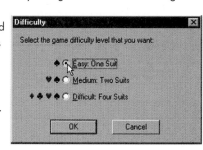

5 Windows Me includes several online diversions, too. Select one of the simple Internet move-based games, such as Checkers. A prompt screen appears before connecting you to the Internet. Click the Play button and the game will connect via your own Internet service provider.

6 Once connected, the game's server locates an opponent who wants to play the same game. Here, the opponent is playing with the white pieces and we will go first. Moving is just a matter of dragging the piece to a new position. Data describing your move is sent via the Internet to your opponent's computer, both boards are updated and the turn switches to your opponent.

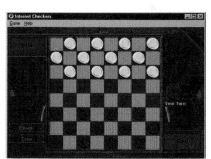

7 Your opponent has said hello – shown in the chat panel at the bottom of the Checkers screen. To select a phrase in reply, click on the box at the bottom of the Checkers screen and choose a suitable response.

PC TIPS

The Pinball game table is fixed as a small 606x460 pixel window. This is too small on large monitors so playing the game at full screen will help you keep track of the ball. Select Full Screen from the Options menu or press [F4] to make the table fill the screen.

Windows Help

Even experienced computer users need help occasionally and the first place they turn to is usually the computer itself.

PC TIPS

Trouble-shooting
One of Windows' Help features is the Troubleshooter. This helps you solve any problems or areas of difficulty which you may frequently encounter involving your computer hardware. For instance, if you are having trouble setting up your modem or printer, the Troubleshooter will take you through the most likely causes step by step (below), hopefully solving the problem (see page 23).

Everyone needs help with Windows at some time, especially when trying to master complex new software. The bulky manuals supplied with some programs are not always the best place to find a quick answer to what may be a relatively simple problem and it can often be like looking for a needle in a haystack. However, when you first load software, a set of Help files, comprehensive enough to rival even the thickest manual, are transferred to your computer.

● Constantly online
The Help available on your computer is known as online Help, not because you have to log on to the Internet, but because it is always available. You can search through the online Help system for a particular subject or for advice on how to use a keyboard or mouse command. You can even type in a simple question such as 'how do I format a paragraph?' and the suggested answer is then displayed. All Windows programs use the [F1] key (near the top left-hand corner of your

keyboard) as an easy way to access Help. Most programs also provide a menu option labelled 'Help' that gives you access to the same Help system as pressing the [F1] key. The reason for the availability of two routes to the Help feature is convenience – if you are typing, you may find it easier to use the keyboard method, or, if you are using your mouse, you may prefer to just point and click on the Help menu instead of moving over to the keyboard.

● Here to help
Once you have got used to using online Help, you will soon find that it is a fast, friendly and convenient way of diagnosing and solving a problem. It will help you learn more about your computer and, now you know that your PC will do its best to make sure you don't get stuck, you can be even more confident in your home computing.

For added convenience, the Help facilities may guide you through a procedure requiring several steps to accomplish it. You can also print out Help text for closer study.

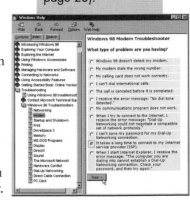

Using Help with Windows

Windows can be a source of confusion for computer users, but it needn't be. Here we show you how to find information about creating files and folders with Windows Help.

1 Click on the Start button in the bottom left corner of the Windows Desktop. Click on the Help option in the middle of the Start menu.

2 The main Windows Help screen appears. From here, there are three ways of looking for information, each accessed by the tabs at the top of the screen. Contents groups information into several main headings, Index lists all the main key words alphabetically and Search offers a powerful way of searching the entire electronic Help library.

3 To find help on a general subject, such as how to use files and folders, look in the Contents page. Click on the Contents tab to see the main headings for the information. Most are illustrated by a closed book icon. Click on the Exploring Your Computer icon.

4 The book icon opens to reveal more books in a sub-list. Click on Files and Folders.

5 Click on Managing Files to see a list of the titles that are available from the Help pages. Click on the Create a folder entry to see the information about creating folders displayed on the right side of the Help window.

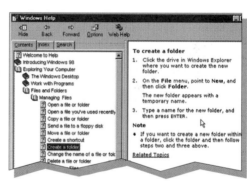

6 There is a faster way of finding the same information. Click on the Index tab of the Windows Help screen. You will see an alphabetical list of all the key words covered. Type in the name of the topic for which you need help ('creating') in the blank box and a list of related Help topics appears in the bottom window, including 'creating folders'. Double-click on this entry to see the full details (as shown in Step 5).

7 The third way of using Help is to search through the manuals by entering a key word. Click on the Search tab and type 'create folder' in the box at the top. Click the List Topics button.

8 Windows looks through its topics and displays items that match the search words at the bottom of the screen. Double-click one to see more information.

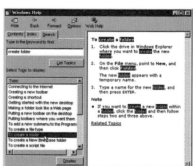

Program Help summed up

All Windows programs use their own Help files, but they all work in a similar way to Windows Help. Here we show you how Help works for two popular Windows programs.

1 Start Calculator by going to the Start button, clicking Programs, then Accessories, then Calculator. We have selected the scientific calculator (by selecting Scientific from the View menu). Press the [F1] key to access Calculator Help.

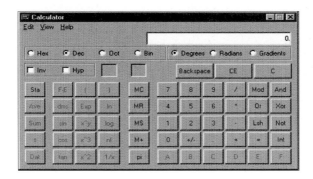

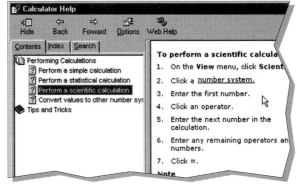

2 The layout of the Calculator Help window looks identical to Windows Help, but the contents are related specifically to Calculator and its functions. There are two books here: Performing Calculations and Tips and Tricks.

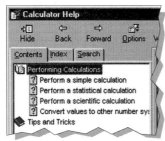

3 Click on Performing Calculations. We want assistance with scientific calculations, so click the Perform a scientific calculation entry. Help will display information on the right in the usual way.

---

1 Some programs, such as WinZip, have a slightly different Help system, with a Find tab instead of Search (below). The first time you click Find, you will see the main screen, which asks you about how Help should handle the information it needs for its files. Select Minimize database size, then click on Next and then click Finish – it usually takes a few seconds to set up.

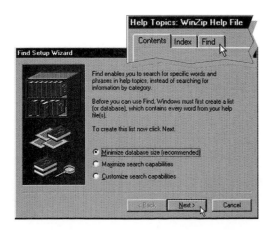

2 Once the database has been created, type a word or phrase into the first box. Matching entries then appear in the centre panel. Next, click on an entry in the centre panel to narrow your search and then double-click on the entry in the lower list.

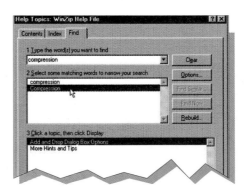

3 A new floating Help window opens up to show details on your choice of topic. To go back to the Find panel, click the Contents button.

Getting out of trouble with Help

It would be useful to have an expert on hand to help you fix problems with your computer whenever they arise, and Windows troubleshooting guides do just that.

1 Printing is a common problem area. The printer either doesn't print exactly what's on the screen or it doesn't print at all. Luckily, there is a troubleshooting guide to help you find out what the problem is. Let's assume that your printer is not printing the whole document. Open Windows Help and click on the Contents tab. Click on Troubleshooting and then click on Windows 98 Troubleshooters.

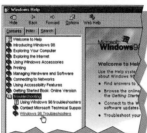

2 The list of options is then presented. The fourth option, Print, looks like the most obvious one to help solve a printer problem, so double-click on it.

3 The Help screen now changes to show the most common printer problem symptoms. Select the symptom that best describes your problem and click on the Next button.

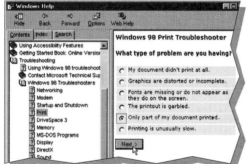

4 When you click on a symptom, the Help program continues to narrow down the possible problems and shows a further screen with more specific advice on it. Read the text and select the option that fits your problem.

5 Help's Troubleshooting guide now displays its first diagnosis of the printer problem. Read through the information and suggestions. Follow the steps it outlines before choosing the option from the bottom of the window.

6 The Help window remains on the screen while you are working through the advice, so you can continue to follow it without taking your eyes off the computer screen or your fingers off the keyboard.

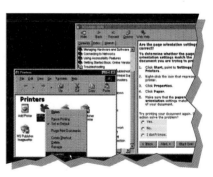

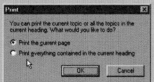
7 In the printer window, the Troubleshooter advises us to check the paper orientation in the printer window. This turns out to be the root of the problem. We had forgotten to change our paper size from Envelope to A4. The Troubleshooter suggests printing again to check if the change works, which it does. The Troubleshooter asks if the problem is fixed; select the Yes option and click the Next button to close the Troubleshooter.

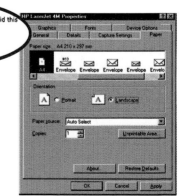

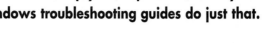

Troubleshooting wizards

Even extremely experienced computer users can encounter software problems. As we have just seen on pages 20-23, Windows' own Help files can usually provide the solutions.

The Help system in Windows 95 was substantially improved for Windows 98 and Windows Me. The Help function is still accessed from the same place on the Start menu, but all other aspects of it have been radically improved. It is now much quicker and easier to search for specific words and phrases within the Help system, and the actual content of the files is more useful, clearer and gives better advice than simply 'refer to your product manufacturer'. Since this is the age of the Internet, it also offers the obligatory online functionality, which means that if the Help system is unable to provide you with a solution, you are automatically taken to online (Web site) resources that can.

● Enter the wizards

One of the biggest changes to the Windows Help system, though, is the introduction of new troubleshooting wizards. These were first seen in Windows 95 as a step-by-step guide to helping with some of the more complex software and hardware problems. However,

they were often short and incomplete, and the range of subjects covered was narrow. Windows has solved all these problems and features a range of troubleshooters ready to help with everything from memory problems to hardware conflicts.

Although they are accessed through the standard Windows Help system, the new Windows Troubleshooters are more useful as they cover a much better and more specific range of problems, rather than giving a general description of how a particular feature or application works. Although each one is different, in terms of size and complexity, there are two main types of troubleshooter.

The first is the smaller and simpler one, as used in the exercise on page 26. Generally, these more basic troubleshooters consist of two or three pages of linked text, offering various solutions to a single area of concern.

Don't despair – Help is at hand. A large number of problems are comprehensively addressed by Windows troubleshooters.

STARTING THE TROUBLESHOOTING WIZARDS

The troubleshooting wizards can be started in a number of ways. Often, when there is a serious problem that Windows is aware of, a wizard will appear automatically. At other times, they will be available as options when installing new hardware or software. But any of the Troubleshooters can also be started manually, as described in the exercise on page 26.

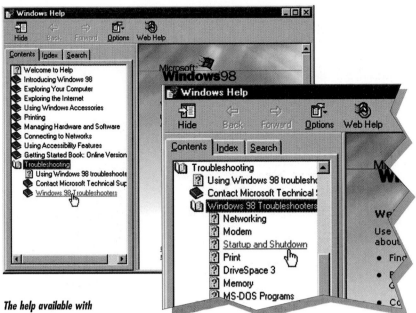

The help available with Windows is extremely wide-ranging. To access the troubleshooting wizards in Windows 98, call up Help and click on the Troubleshooting entry under the Contents tab. Then click the Windows Troubleshooters entry to see the full range.

They cover the more manageable issues, such as insufficient disk space, Windows system file problems and task scheduling. These are not necessarily simple subjects, but they do have a fairly small range of potential problems and areas of confusion.

● **Solving complex problems**
The second type of troubleshooting wizard is much richer and more interactive. While a problem such as too little disk space has only a few basic solutions, others can be much more complex and open-ended. Detecting and solving problems with hardware or networks, for example, can be very difficult without expert advice – and this is just what the longer troubleshooters aim to provide.

These full-length troubleshooters are similar to a questionnaire or multiple-choice form. They start by asking general questions about

the difficulty, for example, 'What is the type of problem you're experiencing with your printer?'. A number of possible responses are given for this question and the one you choose dictates which Help screen you see next. Depending on the complexity of the problem, you will then be shown a series of Help screens according to the symptoms that you describe.

● **No knowledge required**
The troubleshooter assumes no prior technical knowledge on your part and will take you through all the steps given in each potential solution. When you're asked to check the printer driver graphics to see if there's a problem with them, you'll be given a seven point guide on how to do so. By keeping the Help window open on the Desktop at the same time, you can usually follow the steps by referring to the on-screen help. Alternatively, you can simply print it out and proceed using a hard copy. Using the troubleshooter in this way really is just like having your own computer expert on 24-hour stand-by.

Nothing is perfect, however, and although the Windows troubleshooting guides are a great improvement on earlier versions, they cannot always resolve the problem for you. Microsoft have therefore made good use of the Web so that if you have tried all the suggestions and options given without success, further help is available. If a troubleshooter doesn't manage to solve a problem for you, then it will refer you to a useful Web site that might be able to help. As a last resort, it will also show you how and where to contact a Microsoft technician, but you might well find that the real Windows expert is slower to respond than the virtual one.

TROUBLESHOOTING WINDOWS ME

Windows Me includes the same troubleshooters as Windows 98, but you start them up in a slightly different way. To make them easier to find, Microsoft moved the Troubleshooting link, right, to the opening screen. Click on this link and the page changes to show several broad areas; click on one of these to see individual troubleshooters.

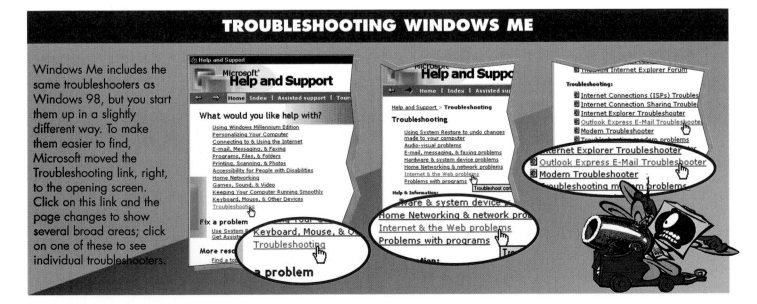

Freeing up disk space

In this exercise we show you how to resolve a problem relating to disk space using the shorter form of troubleshooter. These small troubleshooters act rather like a searchable tips database and tend not to be as interactive as the larger ones.

1 To see a list of the Troubleshooters, use the Start menu and click on Help. The Windows Help window appears on your Desktop.

2 Under the Index tab, begin to type in 'troubleshoot'. The Help file guesses the word from the fisrt few letters, and a list of all the various Troubleshooters and associated Help files will appear before you finish typing.

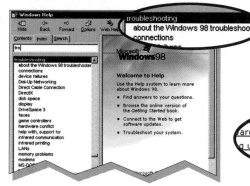

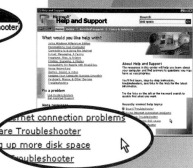

3 Our simulated problem is with disk space, so scroll down the list, highlight that entry and click on the Display button. At this point you might also want to click the Hide button on the toolbar, so that the Troubleshooter is of a more manageable size on-screen.

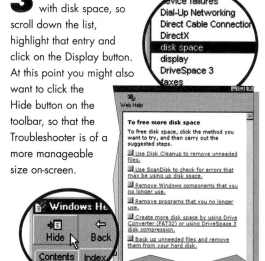

4 Like most of the shorter and less complex troubleshooters, the one to help free up disk space is basically a simple list of HTML-style links. Each link suggests a different course of action for helping with the problem described at the top of the window. In our example we've chosen the first suggestion.

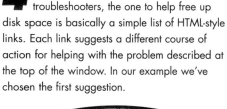

5 Click on the link that you think will assist you best and you'll be shown a single page of help instructions. Usually, there are only six or fewer steps. Don't close the Help window until you are finished and try to keep it visible as you work through it.

6 As you work through the Troubleshooter, you open up other dialog boxes to solve the problem. Where possible, place the windows side by side to make it easy to refer back to the Troubleshooter's advice.

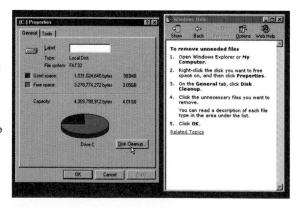

7 When you've finished using this tip, the Troubleshooter contains a link labelled Related Topics. Click on this for an option to jump to Help screens that will provide further assistance. In this case, it tells you of other ways of clearing disk space and how to tell how much space is left on your hard drive.

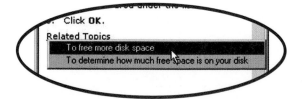

Installing a problem modem

Here we'll use one of the more complex troubleshooters. These often have multiple-choice user inputs that allow you to track down a specific problem. They look different to the basic Help systems, but are just as easy to use.

1 As modem software is quite complex, it can take some time to track down the problem. Bring up Windows Help and type 'troubleshoot' under the Index Tab. Now select the modems Troubleshooter and click Display.

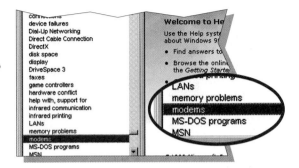

2 The first thing you'll have to do is click on the Click here link to start the Help process. As you'll be answering a series of questions, you need to pay careful attention to the on-screen prompts.

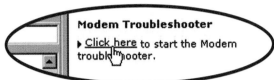

3 Our problem is that Windows is failing to detect the modem, even though it appears to be connected properly. We therefore need to select the first option. Then click the Next button at the bottom of the window – you might need to scroll down to see it.

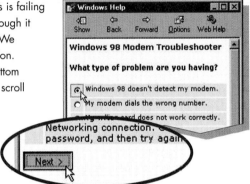

4 The first page of the Troubleshooter covers the basics by telling you to ensure that the modem is installed correctly, according to its operating manual. After doing so you must respond to the question Does this action solve the problem?. This offers you one of three answers used on most pages of the troubleshooters: Yes, No or skip. In our case the answer is No. Then select Next.

5 Now we are told to investigate the possibility of a resource conflict. This is a complex question, but it is well explained by the troubleshooter. As well as showing you how to check for conflicts and how to resolve them, it also gives a number of notes and pointers. We'll skip this step, though, as we know this isn't the problem. Scroll down until you find the buttons at the bottom of the text. Select the skip option and click Next.

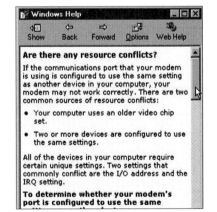

6 We are now presented with another solution. (Note that at the bottom of each troubleshooter page you have the chance to go back to the previous page, or to Start Over. Just click on either of these buttons to do so.) Select the skip option again and click Next to continue.

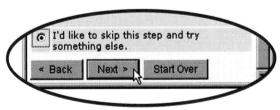

7 The next page is unusual in that it asks you to confirm the presence of a communications port — if this isn't working, then it could well explain what is wrong with your modem. Read through the instructions and select Yes to the question, Is the port present? and then click on Next.

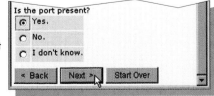

8 The next page of the Troubleshooter solves our problem – we need to install the device manually. Follow the Troubleshooter's advice. Now we are asked if this action has solved the problem. Click Yes and then Next to let Windows know the problem is fixed. Windows then thanks you!

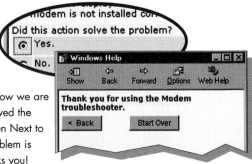

Software

Microsoft®Publisher

Labels: mail merging and printing

Pre-printed labels look smart and professional and are essential if you're sending out a mass mailshot. Here's how to get Word to print labels without wasting time and money.

Mail merging data on to labels and letters is one of the best examples of how you can get your computer to do tedious, repetitive work for you. If you need to send a mailshot to a few dozen people or even more, a mail merge takes care of the bulk of the repetitive work – producing the letters and address labels for you.

The most common mail merge task is creating mail merge letters. Here you combine several variable bits of data – typically names and addresses – with a standard letter to create what appear to be fully personalized letters. Each is individually addressed and, as far as the recipient is concerned, the letter looks just as if it's been written for them alone (see Stage 3 pages 50-53).

Word's mail merge features are also powerful and flexible enough to apply to many other tasks (see Look smart box, on

Ensure your letters get a first-class reception by using Microsoft Word to create professional-looking address labels.

page 30). You can print out a set of labels with your own address, for example, to stick on SAEs or prized possessions, and it's a lot cheaper and quicker than ordering printed labels from a stationery supplier.

The first task in a mailshot is to create a form letter and then merge the names and address data into the letter to produce a batch of personalized letters. You follow almost exactly the same process to print off address labels, one for each letter.

● Mail merge requirements
To mail merge labels, you need a data source document that contains the name and address information you want printed on the labels. While Word is fine as the data source for mail merges to a few dozen people, it isn't the best place to store the data, especially when there is a large amount of it. It's difficult to share this information with other programs because they cannot read the data in the Word table. If

WORD 2000

Word 2000 has most of Word 97's commands, so whichever program you use, future Word exercises in *PCs made easy* will work in both programs. Where there are any differences, we'll highlight the Word 2000 method with this type of box.

LOOK SMART

One of the key benefits of printed address labels is that they give a smart and professional appearance to an envelope. You also avoid the tricky task of printing envelopes (see Stage 3, pages 26-27). In fact, if you regularly send letters to a particular person or company, you can print several of the same addresses on label sheets so that you will have them ready to hand when they are needed.

PC TIPS

Plain paper checking

Before putting your label paper in the printer, print the first page on plain paper. Then, overlay the page on top of your label paper. Hold them up to the light so you can see how the text sits within each label. Allow at least 5mm round the edges for slight variations from one page to the next as they pass through the printer.

you are storing information on more than 20 or 30 people, it's worth using a program that's better suited to storing data, namely a database.

As in a Word data source document, a database program will store the address information for your labels as a table of data. The data is split into rows called records – one record per person in most cases – and each record is split into fields: first name, last name, street address and so on. This well-defined structure is easy for Word to access and place in a mail merge document, such as a set of labels. However, the difference is that data is much easier for Word to handle when it's in a proper database.

● **Creating and using an Excel database**

To create a database in Excel, you just use the spreadsheet columns for fields and add one row for each person. You save the database as

a normal Excel spreadsheet and then open it from Word to do the mail merge (see page 33). Word and Excel work very well together and Word can use an Excel data store as easily as it can one of its own. Because the data is in Excel, its spreadsheet facilities are available should you wish to make use of the data in ways other than for a mail merge.

● **Label printer options**

There are two approaches to label printing. You can opt for a dedicated label printer (see Stage 4, page 106-107) which, because it uses a continuous reel of individual labels, allows you to print just the labels you need without any wastage. The alternative is to use A4 sheets of labels on backing sheets in your printer. This leads to a little wastage, as there are likely to be several unused labels after each print run, but most people prefer to avoid the extra outlay on a dedicated label printer.

Choosing the right labels

Label paper comes in several sizes, and the shapes and sizes of the labels themselves vary widely. It's not worth buying a box of label paper until you're sure you can use it without undue fuss and bother.

PRINTING LABELS FROM Word used to involve a great deal of trial and error, and inevitably a lot of wasted labels. However, with each new version of Word, Microsoft has added valuable refinements to label printing to rectify such problems. Now Word has an in-built knowledge of the size, shape and layout of many popular types and brands of label.

You can save yourself a lot of trouble if you check to see which types of labels Word knows and then choose the shape and size that best matches your needs. To see what's available, bring up the Label Options dialog box (see Steps 4 and 5 on page 32).

As you click on each type of label in the Product number panel, the Label information area shows the important dimensions. Use these as a guide to the type of label you need.

If you decide to choose a label size that doesn't conform to the dimensions of any of the products that Word knows, you can take your own measurements and then type these in yourself. Click on the New Label button in the Label Options dialog box and use the dialog box that appears to define your labels. The dialog box lists all the measurements that Word needs to know before it is able to print the labels properly.

There are labels designed for many different purposes. Browse through a stationery catalogue and check Word's label lists in the Label Options dialog box to find a suitable match.

You can tell Word about the dimensions and layout of any labels it doesn't already know in the New Custom laser dialog box (right). This has a preview window where you can see what effects the dimensions you key in to the various boxes will have on the label you are specifying.

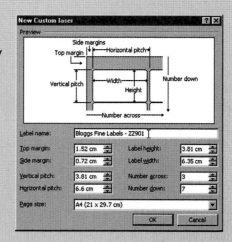

Printing multiple copies of one label

Even if you never have to do a mass mailshot, there are plenty of ways to make good use of Word's label printing features – here we show you how to pre-print your own address labels.

1 Start a new Word document and type in your address. Use Word's formatting tools to give it the font and style you want.

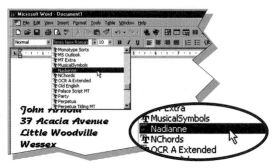

2 Next select the whole address and then choose the Envelopes and Labels command from the Tools menu.

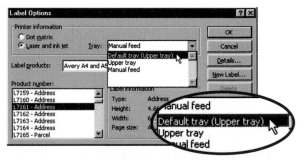

3 Click the Labels tab of the dialog box. The Address panel shows the address you have selected. Make sure that the Full page of the same label option is selected in the Print section near the bottom of the dialog box.

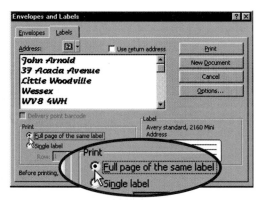

4 You must now tell Word what type of label paper you are using. Click the Label picture at the bottom right of the dialog box to bring up the Label Options dialog box and select the brand of label you have bought (see Choosing the right labels box, page 31).

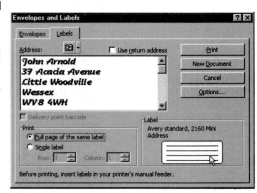

5 Once you have chosen the right brand of label, scroll down the Product number list on the left and select the code name or number for the labels (you should find it printed on the packaging of the labels).

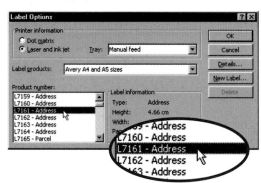

6 Now insert the labels into your printer's manual **feed** tray or slot (see Stage 2, page 95). If you're not **sure** which this is, you can use the printer's normal paper **tray** instead. Place the paper in the tray and then use the Tray list box in the Printer information section to select it. Click on OK to continue.

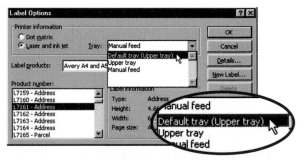

7 Finally, click the Print button in the Envelopes and Labels dialog box to start the print job.

INKJETS AND LABELS

If you use an inkjet printer, you should think twice before using it for address labels. Many inkjets use water-soluble inks and you may find that your address information is susceptible to smudging. Experiment with some printed labels first before sending them out. Spraying them with some fixing spray from an artist's shop might protect them from smudging.

Mail merging labels from Excel data

By combining Word's mail merge facilities with Excel's data handling power, you can create instant labels for all manner of mailshots.

1 Open Excel and create a mini-database document (see Stage 3, pages 56-57). Here we've got columns for a club, including membership numbers, names, addresses and phone numbers. Save the document and close Excel.

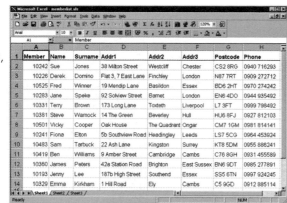

2 Open Word and click Mail Merge in the Tools menu. In the Mail Merge Helper dialog box, click on the Create button and select Mailing Labels.

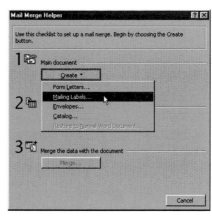

3 Click the Active Window button when Word asks which document to use.

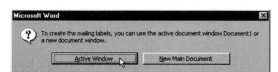

4 Now click on the Get Data button and select Open Data Source. Select your Excel mini-database and click the Open button. If Word asks if you want the entire spreadsheet, click the OK button.

5 Click the Set Up Main Document button when Word asks and then select the right brand and code number of label (see Steps 4 and 5 on the previous page). Click OK when you've done this.

6 Now choose the merge fields you want on your labels. Click the Insert Merge Field button, and select the first name field. It is then added to the Sample label box. Select each field in turn, adding a space between any two fields on one line and pressing the [Enter] key to start a new line. Click the OK button when you have finished.

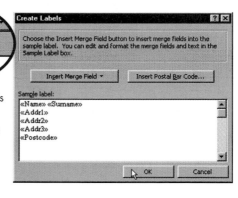

7 Now that all the preparation is done, click the Merge button in the Mail Merge Helper dialog box.

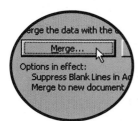

8 To send the merged labels directly to your printer, select Printer in the Merge to box, and then click the Merge button. The usual Word Print dialog box appears. Make sure the labels are inserted in the printer correctly and press the Print button to start printing your labels.

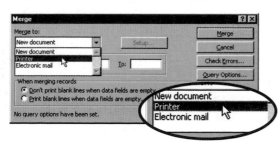

PC TIPS

Changing typeface

If you want to use a bolder typeface or larger type size on your mail-merged labels, you can change the setting in the Create Labels dialog box (see Step 6). Select all the field names you want to format and right-click on the highlighted text. Select Font from the pop-up menu to get access to the other typefaces available.

Using custom dictionaries

Are you irritated by Word's spell checker querying words that are correct? If you use a specialized vocabulary or a foreign language in your work you'll want to take advantage of Word's Custom Dictionary features.

We've already seen how efficiently Word's spelling and grammar features work (see Stage 2, pages 30-33) and how they can polish up not just your spelling, but also your style. However, not even a spell checker as extensive as Word's is capable of containing every single word you might need to use.

It is for this reason that Word's spelling and grammar checking facility also has a built-in Custom Dictionary to which you can add words that are not already in the spell checker's database. If you find the spell checker queries words that you use frequently, it's well worth taking the time to add them to the dictionary, leaving Word to concentrate on correcting the genuine spelling mistakes.

● What to add?

There are some obvious things you might want to add to the default Custom Dictionary. These include: names of people or places that occur regularly in your documents or correspondence; initials or acronyms relating to your work or study, such as MUFC, for example, if you were writing about Manchester United Football Club; and terms peculiar to a profession or trade, such as building, medicine or law.

It can also be handy to create a custom dictionary for a specialist subject. In our step-by-step exercise opposite we've used the example of someone who is writing a history project on World War I, which necessarily involves a lot of foreign place names and personalities.

Once names, such as Eckhert, or place names, such as Reichstag, have been added to the custom dictionary, Word's basic spelling checker will no longer flag these common items.

Don't be restricted by Word's standard dictionary. You can add individual words to cater for your own specialist subject, or even a complete, ready-made foreign-language dictionary.

● Specialized dictionaries

When it comes to writing highly technical documents, a specialized custom dictionary is essential. If you don't want to create your own, you can buy a ready-made specialized one. Many such products exist, especially for legal, medical and scientific use.

A good place to look for technical dictionaries that can be used with Word is at www.worldlanguage.com. If you do a lot of word processing in a foreign language, you will almost certainly need an additional dictionary in that language. Once installed, this will work like any other custom dictionary you create. The company that created Word's spell checker, Alki Software, has a site with details of its dictionaries (www.proofing.com). Expect to pay around £60 for a foreign-language dictionary.

PC TIPS

Sharing

If you share your computer with other people, it's quite possible that the words you add for your documents are not much use for others. Fortunately, Word allows you to create several custom dictionaries. Each person can save a dictionary under his or her own name and then activate the preferred dictionary when spell checking.

Creating and using a custom dictionary

You don't have to buy a custom dictionary to make the most of Word's powerful spell-checking. In this example, we create our own dictionary to help with a project involving foreign place names.

HERE WE'LL SHOW you how to create a custom dictionary for use with a history project on the origins of World War I. As this involves lots of foreign place names and names of personalities, a custom dictionary will stop Word from questioning words we know are correct. We've used a fairly long text here – but you can start your own custom dictionary with a shorter text, and then add to it each time you use new words.

1 Open a Word document containing words that you would like to add to your new custom dictionary. From the Tools menu, select Options.

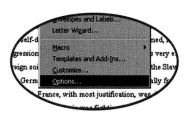

2 Click the Spelling & Grammar tab in the Options dialog box and then click the Dictionaries button.

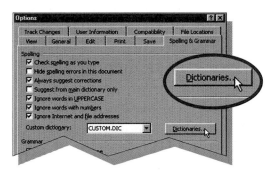

3 The Custom Dictionaries dialog box shows the dictionaries on your computer. You'll most likely see a single CUSTOM.DIC entry. This is the default custom dictionary that every computer has. Click the New button.

4 Word needs you to assign a name to your custom dictionary. Type it in the File name box and then click on the Save button.

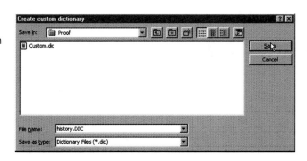

5 You'll now see your dictionary listed. Turn off all other dictionaries listed here by unticking the box next to their name. A message box warns you that you have deselected the first dictionary on the list. You can ignore this message. Press the OK button to return to your document.

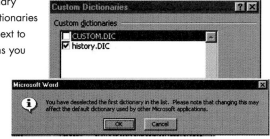

6 Spell check your text by pressing the [F7] key. Word starts to use your custom dictionary, although there are no words in it yet. As you come across queried words which you know are correct, click the Add button to add them to your new dictionary. Note: be wary of accidentally pressing the Add button for any words that really are misspelt.

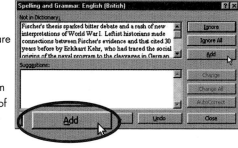

7 You can check that the dictionary is now working properly by closing your Word document, reopening it and running the spell check again. The checker will not query any of the words you added in Step 6.

Additional wizards and templates

There are many ways to work faster and smarter with Word. With wizards and templates you can easily create more professional-looking documents.

We have introduced Word's wizards and templates earlier in the course. In Stage 3, pages 30-33, for instance, we used Word's newsletter Wizard to create a great-looking newsletter in just a few simple steps.

With a wizard, a series of dialog boxes asks you to make multiple-choice selections, typing in your own information where relevant. This is then used to create the appropriate type of document with important information already in place.

A template, on the other hand, is simply a special kind of pre-prepared document. Word comes with many such template documents – for letters, memos, invoices and so on – into which you can enter your own information. While wizards and templates are quite different, they both aim to save you time and to help you create attractive finished documents. Here we look at both templates and wizards together, and see how we can add even more of them to Word.

● Advice and advanced features

A great thing about templates and wizards is that not only do they make the creation and formatting of complex documents straightforward, but they often give plenty of excellent advice. This advice is usually included as the dummy text of the document. Once you have read the advice, you simply select it, then replace it with the text you really want to include in your document. The newsletter Wizard, for example, gives advice

about the effective use of headings, boxes and so on. Some templates use advanced Word features that you might not usually employ. These include fields and macros (see Stage 4, pages 38-41 and Stage 5, pages 30-37 respectively). Both these features can give a useful element of automation to documents. A template can even include a formula to perform calculations in a table of figures automatically.

● Extra wizards and templates

Although Word comes with a wide range of wizards and templates to make your life easier, the full selection can be hard to find.

This is due to the Typical install option with which Word has been copied to the hard disks of most computers.

There are more wizards and templates available to you than the few that are installed by default on your hard disk. We show you where to find them.

WORD 2000

If you've already got Word 2000, using uninstalled templates is very easy. Even if the template you want was not installed when you first ran Word 2000, once you select the template, the program asks you to insert the CD-ROM into your PC and copies over the files.

This installation option doesn't include everything from the original CD-ROM. To install some files, you must either make the selection manually at the time of the original installation; add them subsequently (we show you how to below); or, in some cases, access them directly from the CD-ROM itself.

The exact number and types of templates might also vary from CD-ROM to CD-ROM, depending on the date it was produced by Microsoft. If your computer came with Microsoft Office, rather than Microsoft Word alone, you will also have other templates and wizards. On the Office CD-ROM there are several useful templates you must install

manually from the CD-ROM's ValuPack folder (see Installing templates and wizards from CD-ROM box, below).

● Files from the Internet

There are yet more templates and wizards, as well as improved versions of the originals, posted on the Microsoft Web site (see page 39). Although the site isn't the easiest to navigate, largely due to its sheer size, and the fact that some pages originally created for Word 97 have been moved since the launch of Word 2000, if you persevere with the on-site search engine, you can find a lot of useful files for many versions of Word.

Installing templates and wizards from CD-ROM

This exercise will ensure that you have all the available wizards and templates installed in your version of Word. If you later decide that you no longer want them, you can always delete them.

1 Bring up the Add/Remove Program Properties dialog box (see Stage 3, pages 18-21). Under the first tab, Install/Uninstall, select Microsoft Word 97 and press Add/Remove.

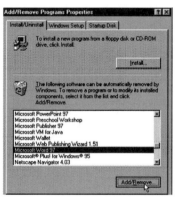

2 Ensure you have your CD-ROM in the CD-ROM drive before you click the Add/Remove button in the next dialog box.

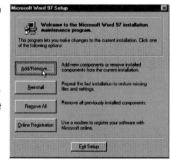

PC TIPS

Versions

Depending on the version of Word or Office that you have, your CD-ROM may contain extra templates. Explore the CDs for folders named TEMPLATE or Template. You can open up individual templates directly by double-clicking on them, or copy them to the Templates folder of your hard disk to make them appear in the New dialog box.

3 If there are wizards and templates as yet uninstalled on your PC, the tick box next to the Wizards and Templates entry will be grey (below). Select the entry and press the Change Option button. (If the box is white and ticked, you already have all the wizards and templates installed; press the Cancel button and close the Add/Remove Programs dialog box.)

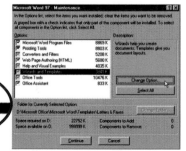

4 You can now see a list of all the wizards and templates. Click the Select All button and click OK. After the files have been copied to your hard disk, close the Add/Remove Programs dialog box.

5 The new templates and wizards appear in Word's New dialog box, arranged into groups according to the folders copied to the hard disk.

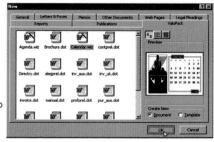

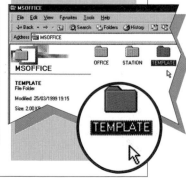

Introducing the extra templates and wizards

Here's a breakdown of extra wizards (.wiz files) and templates (.dot files) that you'll be able to use after following the exercise on page 37.

Calendar.wiz

As its name suggests, this creates a calendar for you: anything from a single month to a whole year and in a choice of three styles.

Thesis.dot

The main purpose of this template is to remind you what to include in your thesis.

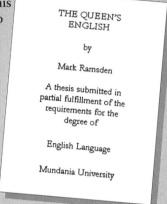

PC TIPS

Macro alert

Opening up some templates or wizards generates a dialog box that warns you of the possible dangers of macros. This is because Word macros are powerful enough to be destructive as well as creative; some virus writers use macros to create their viruses. Word warns you whenever it opens a document or template containing a macro, just to be on the safe side. As long as the file is from a reputable source, such as the Microsoft CD-ROM itself, click the Enable Macro button and proceed. If in doubt, press the Disable Macro button (below), but be prepared for some of the template's automated features to be missing.

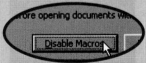

Brochure.dot

This is a handy and attractive template for producing A4 fold-out brochures (such as take-away menus); the body text includes plenty of formatting and general advice.

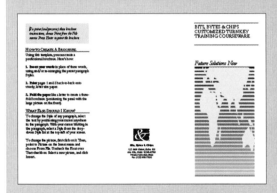

Contprel.dot, Elegprel.dot and Profprel.dot

These supply press-release templates, in the classic Microsoft Contemporary, Elegant and Professional styles (see Stage 5, page 43).

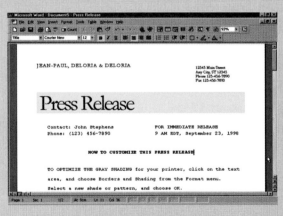

Manual.dot

This is an impressive template for creating manuals and instruction books. It includes cover, acknowledgments, and contents pages. There are also graphics, margins, boxes, drop text – and lots of advice.

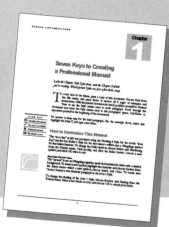

Agenda.wiz

This creates an organized agenda for meetings, including venue, agenda titles, the name of the person who called the meeting, space for minutes, and so on.

Get wizards and templates from the Web

Whatever version of Word you use, you can visit the Microsoft Web site and browse through lots of free-to-download templates and wizards.

1 Microsoft has a large download area on its Web site, with a search engine to make locating files easy. Start your Web browser and type www.microsoft.com/ downloads/search.asp into the Address box and you'll be taken to the microsoft.com Download Center.

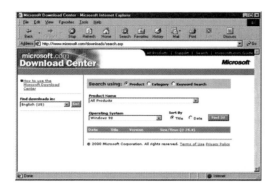

2 Select your version of Word from the Product Name list box in the centre of the page (Microsoft lists the most popular versions of its programs here – past and present). Press the Find It button (inset).

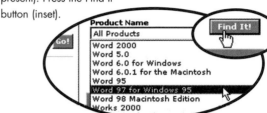

3 Within a few moments, the page expands to show the pages that match your search. Browse through the list and look for interesting or recent entries. Click on a link if it seems useful.

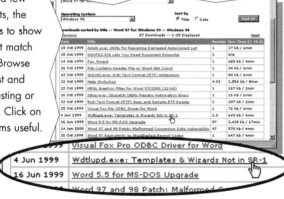

4 The next page describes the contents of the downloadable file and contains a link to start the download. When you're sure that this is the template you want, click on the link (inset).

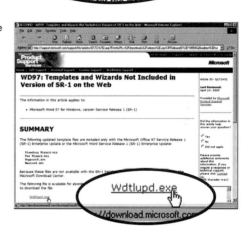

5 In the first dialog box that appears, select the Save this program to disk option (inset) and click OK. Then use the Save As dialog box to save the file to a folder on your hard disk drive.

6 When you've finished downloading, disconnect from the Internet and double-click on the file you downloaded (inset). In this example, it's best to extract the files into a temporary folder. Click the Browse button and use the Browse for Folder window to select a suitable folder.

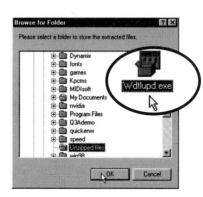

7 Depending on the download you have chosen, you might find a text file containing instructions for installing and/or using the templates (.dot files) and wizards (.wiz files) you have downloaded. In this example you simply copy the files to Word's template folder. One of the files is a text file on how to use the templates.

UPDATING DIRECT FROM WORD 2000

If you are using Word 2000, select the Office on the Web command from Word's Help menu to take you to the Microsoft Office Update page. Click the Downloads link to find the templates and wizards. The full set of updates, with release dates, are listed. Click on the links to get the new files you want; you'll find things like Word 2000 versions of some of the templates that were left out in the Word 97 to Word 2000 upgrade.

Creating great logos

You might not expect a word processor to deliver great graphics results, but with a little exploration and experimentation, you'll find that the WordArt functions Word offers are capable of creating useful and professional–looking logos.

If you have a dedicated design package such as CorelDRAW on your computer, you are less likely to use Word for a major design or layout project. But if you don't have CorelDRAW, or if you want to create something quickly and easily and integrate it within the one program, Word provides a solid range of features. There are also a couple of useful extras, such as a range of fills and textures and some excellent 3D modelling tools.

We've touched on most of Word's drawing tools before (see Stage 3, pages 46-49), but here we're going to put that information into practice in the following exercises. As always, we will give you general design pointers as well as introducing techniques used by graphic artists for designing logos.

Some logos can look quite simple, but that's often the point. The most effective and successful logos tend to have a straightforward, but strong, central idea and bold use of colour, rather than lots of technical wizardry and complex graphics.

● **What the papers say**

As an interesting side exercise, rummage through a magazine or a newspaper and, using a couple of pieces of paper to mask off the rest of the page, examine a famous logo. You might be surprised at just how little you need to see of the image in order to recognize it: for example, just the spindly swirls of Coke; the join of McDonalds' golden arches; or the blue stripes of IBM are enough to make the connection. Some logos almost seem to take over certain typefaces: put any text into a bold, italic **sans serif** face, and you are reminded of Microsoft. All this is partly due

Although it's useful to have a specialist graphics package, such as CorelDRAW, you can create exciting and colourful documents with Microsoft Word.

to ubiquitous advertising, of course, but it's also a product of strong, relevant design.

There's much common sense in the way logos work. The IBM, McDonalds and Coke logos all use typography that reflects the nature of the company and its products: the solid, but slightly exotic swirl of Coke's letters; the serious and modern IBM typeface; and the fairy-tale tinge of McDonalds. But typography is by no means everything and in our two examples, we include a range of design options. Bear in mind that in both cases, the designs are flexible: you could easily do away with the background material and just use the words themselves, according to your needs or your printing limitations. Remember, though, that your logo should

WHAT IT MEANS

SANS SERIF

This is the name given to those typefaces without the subtle embellishments at the ends of the strokes that make up a letter, known as serifs. This box text is in a serif face (Sabon), but the headline of this article is in a sans serif typeface (Futura).

always be consistent, and you shouldn't have too many variations on a theme. It is also a good idea to keep the style of the defining text the same. In our exercise below we introduce 3D modelling and overleaf we use a table and WordArt to create a logo for a fictitious French restaurant. In the exercise on page 43, we've experimented with various

textures and shapes to create a classic design for our own (also fictitious) football team, called the Ravenscourt Parkas.

We looked at the use of clip art in Stage 1, page 46, however don't forget that you are not restricted to the clip art provided by Microsoft. You can also download suitable images from the Internet.

3D modelling

One of the most surprising of Word's functions is its excellent 3D modelling tool, which can be applied to any single object. Here we're going to introduce its basic functions by rendering a map of France in 3D. See the exercise overleaf for where to find this map file.

1 Click on the object you plan to model (the map of France, in this case), then click on the 3D icon on the far right of the Drawing toolbar and select 3-D Settings.

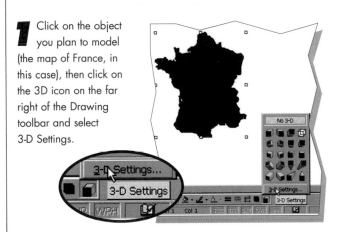

2 A new 3-D Settings toolbar appears. Click once on the Tilt Left button on the toolbar (inset) and the map will rotate to generate a 3D image. Use the horizontal rotate button on the toolbar and gently adjust it until the map resembles the image here.

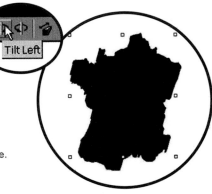

3 Click the Lighting button and then choose the Bright option together with the top-left light source, indicated by an angled lamp, as shown here.

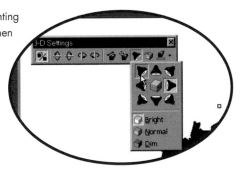

4 Click on the Surface icon, indicated by a box, and select Plastic from the drop-down menu.

5 Click the arrow to the right of the 3D-Color button and select a colour.

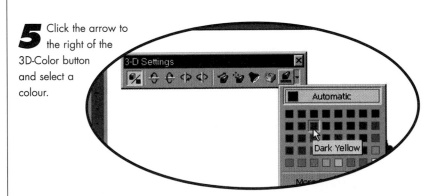

6 Now the map has an attractive, moulded 3D appearance.

Creating your first logo

You'll need the Drawing toolbar for this exercise. Select it from the main toolbar or the Toolbars sub-menu under View (see Stage 3, pages 46-49).

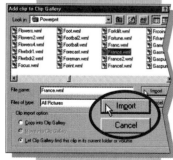

1 Add a table to a blank Word document (see Stage 6, pages 44-47), and then select Table and Borders from the Toolbars sub-menu on the View menu. Use the toolbar to add colour to the table to create a French 'flag', similar to that shown below.

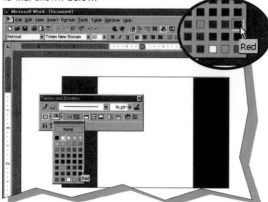

2 Insert a clip art picture (see Stage1, page 46). Here we've used a map of France from the Maps – International category (if it's not there, see PC Tips box, left).

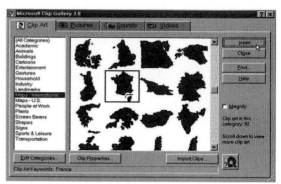

3 Bring up the Format Picture dialog box by selecting Borders and Shading from the Format menu. Click on the Wrapping tab. Change the Wrapping style setting to None and click the OK button.

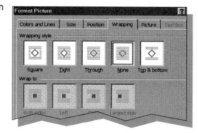

4 To tidy up the map, right-click on it and select Ungroup from the Grouping sub-menu option that appears when you right-click on the picture. Click on the island at the bottom right and press the [Del] key. Do the same for the line above the now-deleted island so that you are left with mainland France only.

5 Resize the map by dragging one of the corners (hold down the [Shift] key to keep the proportions correct). Place it in the bottom-right corner of the white stripe of the 'flag' table.

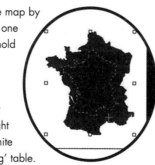

6 Bring up the WordArt Gallery dialog box (see Stage 1, page 45). Select a curved type icon and click OK. Type the name of your restaurant – Josephine's – and select a suitable typeface and size, then click OK.

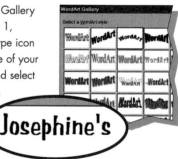

7 Rotate your text so that it sits above and to the left of your map icon. Repeat Step 6 for the second line of text – Le petit Paris – but set it in a smaller point size, and rotate this so that it sits between the name and the map.

8 Finally, insert another suitable piece of clip art, such as the Eiffel Tower, and place it over the position of Paris on the map.

Creating a club emblem

In this exercise, we're going to use Word's preset shapes and textures to create a classic, fabric-style badge for our fictitious football club, the Ravenscourt Parkas.

1 Open a new document and click on the Drawing toolbar's AutoShapes button. Choose Block Arrows and Pentagon. Place the shape on the page by clicking on it, then dragging it with the mouse. Click the Free Rotate tool (inset) until the shape is vertical (right).

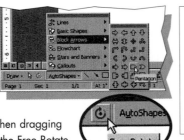

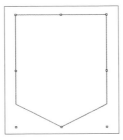

2 Bring up the Fill Effects dialog box (see Stage 3, pages 48-49). Click the Texture tab, select the Denim pattern and click the OK button.

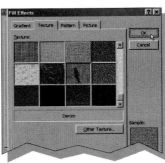

3 Bring up the Format AutoShape dialog box via the Format menu. Click on the Colors and Lines tab and choose a contrasting colour for the outline of a new shape. Choose a heavier line weight – such as 2.25pt – and click the OK button.

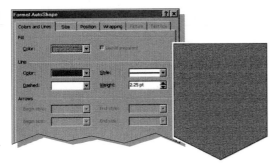

4 Use the AutoShapes menu on the Drawing toolbar to select the Stars and Banners option and click on the second shape to draw an explosion on the top half of the badge.

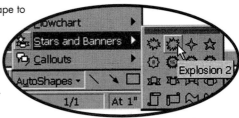

5 Follow Steps 2 and 3 again to change the texture fill to Canvas and select an orange, dashed, 0.5pt line. Click the OK button.

6 Use WordArt (see Stage 1, page 45) to add a line of text for the name of your football team. Change the texture fill to Purple mesh, and, as in Step 5, apply an orange, broken border.

PC TIPS

You can bring up the Format WordArt dialog box directly from the button on the WordArt toolbar.

7 From the AutoShapes menu on the Drawing toolbar, select the Stars and Banners option (see Step 4). Click on one of the ribbon-shaped banners from the third row to add a ribbon across the bottom of the badge. Then add a Purple mesh texture fill and give it a deep blue border.

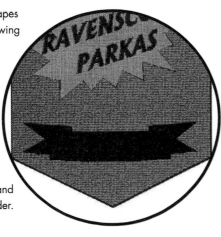

8 Finally, choose a motto for your team and add it to the ribbon with WordArt (as in Step 6). Give it a suitable patterned fill and line style.

Adding watermarks

If you want to add a touch of distinction to documents – or get across a subtle, but unmissable, message – try adding a watermark.

H old up a sheet of good-quality writing or art paper to the light and the chances are that you'll see a distinguishing mark – either a picture, text or a combination of both – in the paper. Watermarks, which date from the 13th century, are one of the oldest forms of branding. They let you know precisely who made the paper and what kind of paper it is. The presence of a watermark is thought to add an elegant touch of class to paper. Watermarks are also used for the discouragement and detection of forgery.

Microsoft Word lets you add the computer equivalent of a watermark to your documents and templates. It appears as a faint background to the page. Word's watermarks are not designed to be used in exactly the same way as the traditional watermark; instead, they enable you to create a graphic or text message that faintly underlies your document. You can create a simple text watermark, import some clip art and other images, or you can use WordArt if you want to create more extravagant text effects.

● **Practical watermarks**
There's a wide range of circumstances in which you might find a watermark a useful, rather than just a decorative, device (although, of course, there's nothing to stop you using a watermark as a purely decorative element). A

Add style to your documents with your own tailor-made watermark.

VIEWING IT

A watermark is inserted into a document via the Header and Footer commands. This means it appears on the printed page and in Print Preview and Page Layout views, but not in Normal view.

club, business or even an individual might want to add some subtle background graphic impact to their pages with the use of a watermark graphic or logo (see the exercise on page 46 for an example of this kind of use). For instance, you could take your company logo and put it on your letterhead document template as a watermark so that it appears faintly on every page.

A more practical use might be to place a watermark behind a list of things you are selling, such as paintings or craft items, where you want the entire list to act as a guide to viewers, indicating also when a particular item is no longer available. In this case you could simply create a watermark saying 'Sold', make it faint but legible, copy it and position it underneath the relevant items, then update and print out the list as and when needed. At first, the way watermarks are

created and used can seem a little odd, since you have to create them through Word's Header and Footer feature. However, unlike most things you put in Headers or Footers, the watermark is not constrained to a position at the top or bottom of the page. You can move it wherever you want. You can even combine text and graphic watermarks by inserting an image, adding some text and then positioning them both exactly where you like.

● **Two methods**
The method for creating a watermark depends on whether it is a graphic or a text item (note, too, that Word treats WordArt as a graphic). In our first exercise, we'll cover the basics by adding a graphic to a club letter. In the second exercise, on page 47, we'll use text that creates an official look for a memo.

Making watermarks with WordArt

Don't forget about the power of WordArt. Employed tastefully, it can be an effective way of getting a message across when you are using a watermark.

INSERTING A PIECE of WordArt instead of normal text can give you many more special effects for your watermark. Text in WordArt can be edited in much the same way as you can edit normal text, altering the typeface, size, emphasis and so on, but WordArt also gives you an interesting range of different fills and text rotations to play with. If you want to use WordArt to create your watermark, follow the procedure in the exercise on the next page for using graphics, then edit the text and the effects you want with WordArt (see Stage 1, page 45). In the case of the exercise on page 47, you might feel that the 'Confidential' stamp would have more impact if it ran diagonally across the page. With WordArt it is simple to rotate text. You can also use special colour fills if you print your work out on a colour inkjet printer.

It's easy to rotate text in WordArt. Pick an angle for the watermark so that it stands out without detracting from the main text.

Beware of making a WordArt watermark too intrusive as this will impinge on the legibility of the document (left).

However, do be wary of going over the top when using the special effects that WordArt can produce. Many of them are great fun but inappropriate for any document that has a serious purpose. It is definitely worth experimenting with watermarks, as you might find something that works very well for your purpose.

Subtle effects can be achieved using WordArt and a colour printer.

Creating a watermark with an imported graphic

In this exercise we'll show you how to use a simple clip-art sport image and add it to a letter from the secretary of an athletics club.

1 Open a suitable Word document and select the Header and Footer command from the View menu to bring up the Header and Footer toolbar (see Stage 2, pages 34-35).

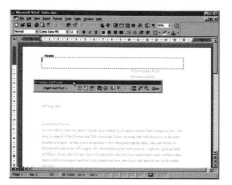

2 Choose a picture by going to the Insert menu, selecting Picture and then Clip Art. We've opted for the runner from the Sports & Leisure section.

3 The picture appears in the document, stretching the Header area. To make alterations to the picture, select the Picture toolbar from the Toolbars sub-menu on the View menu.

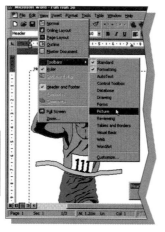

4 Start by resizing the picture, by dragging its handles, to make it considerably smaller.

5 When you're happy with the picture's size, drag it to the position you want. We've chosen to put it in the centre, just below the address line.

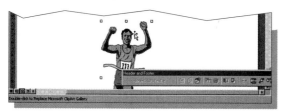

6 To make the image fainter, click on the Image Control button on the Picture toolbar and select Watermark from the pop-up options. This gives the image the right brightness and contrast settings.

7 The main text of the letter has disappeared below this image. To bring it back to overlie the image of the athlete, you must turn off text wrapping. Click on the Text Wrapping button on the Picture toolbar and select None from the drop-down list.

8 The text now flows over the watermark image, which is faint enough for the text to be clearly legible but also strong enough to make its visual point.

Creating a text watermark

Now we want to add an unmistakable warning to an important and confidential memo in such a way that it doesn't interfere with the legibility of the memo's text.

1 Open your document and select Header and Footer from the View menu to show the Header and Footer areas. Select Text Box from the Insert menu.

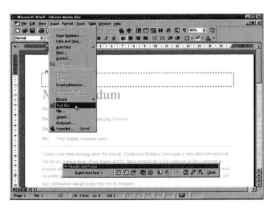

2 The mouse pointer changes to a crosshair. Drag a rectangular area for the text watermark.

3 Type the word CONFIDENTIAL into the text box, selecting a suitable typeface, size and formatting via Word's toolbar buttons.

4 Next, drag the box to a suitable position on the page layout.

5 There's no automatic way to make text faint enough to be a watermark – you must do it yourself. Select the text and use the Font Color button from the Drawing toolbar to change it to Gray-25%.

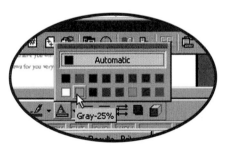

6 To get rid of the text box outline, click on the Line Color button on the Drawing toolbar and select No Line.

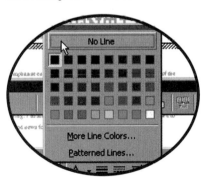

7 Switch to Page Layout mode to see the full effect of your watermark. You'll now have an unmissable message which nevertheless does not interfere with the legibility of the main text.

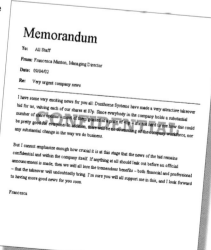

PC TIPS

One page only

Adding a watermark through Word's Headers and Footers options places the watermark on every page. There might be times when you only want a watermark on the first page. The simplest way to do this is to insert a picture without using the Header and Footer view shown in Step 1. Instead, insert a picture or text box in Page Layout view and format as in Steps 5 and 6. Right-click on it (on the edge if it's a text box) and then select the Send Behind Text command from the Order menu.

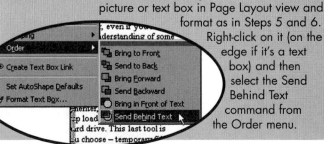

Adding comments

You can add comments to a printed document by just writing on it. But if you make use of Word's facility for adding comments, you won't have to struggle to decipher difficult handwriting or worry about losing the hard copy with vital notes on it.

It's often the case that we want one or more people to read and make comments on our documents before they are finalised. This is not simply because sometimes we may lack confidence in our writing ability. Rather, it is a reflection of the fact that in the modern world much of our work – and even many of our education or leisure activities – is a collaborative process, requiring consensus and agreement.

● **Collaborative and individual computing**
In the past, input from other people often involved illegible handwriting on several paper copies of a document. Word can change all that. It has powerful tools that allow multiple users to add comments and changes to documents without affecting the original. It's then a simple process for an author to accept or reject the suggestions or changes made. This facility assumes even more importance when you consider that many people work at a distance from other colleagues, using email from remote workstations, or in large offices connected through computer networks.

You can email a document to several people, who can then email it back with their own comments or changes, all without a sheet of paper in sight. However, the ability to add comments to documents can be extremely useful even if you're working entirely on your own. You might simply want to insert reminders to yourself about certain points such as: 'Check these figures with Madge in Accounts', 'Get quotation from Oxford Dictionary in school library' and so on. When you've dealt with these points, your comments can simply be deleted from the file, leaving the finished document.

● **Minimal confusion**
The way in which Word inserts comments in documents means that any possible confusion is kept to a minimum. The original text remains perfectly readable and you can view the comments altogether, either in a separate part of the Word window or through pop-up text boxes that appear over the words and phrases to which the comments relate. These are highlighted in the original document so that you can spot them easily.

For collaborative documents, where it's important to see who made which comment, the name or initials of the writer accompanies the comment, appearing in brackets. If there are comments from several people, you can choose to see only those comments made by a particular person. This helps to make sure that you quickly focus on the comments that are most important or relevant.

You don't have to be a professional to use Comments – even a family letter or homework could benefit from a read-through by friends or family.

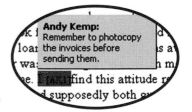

Comments inserted in a Word document are indicated by highlighted text. Just point at the highlight with the mouse pointer to reveal the comment.

Inserting comments in documents

Here we add comments to an essay on the legal profession. Any Word document you have on your computer will demonstrate the principles equally well.

1 Word uses your intitials from its User Information when adding comments. It's best to check this first. Start Word and select Options from the Tools menu. Click the User Information tab in the Options dialog box and make sure your name and initials are correct. Click the OK button. Then put the text insertion point next to the text you want to comment on and select Comment from the Insert menu.

2 The word is highlighted and is followed by the initials of the commentator, in brackets. At the same time, your screen is split horizontally and the Comments panel appears, with the reviewer's initials. Type in a comment.

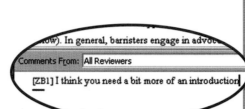

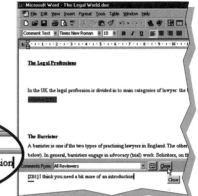

3 Insert another comment in another part of the document by following the same procedure as in Steps 1 and 2. The initials are followed by '2' to show that this is the second comment in the sequence. Click on the Close button on the bar that divides the Comments panel from the main text window.

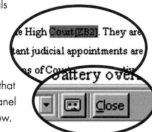

4 The Word window reverts to its normal size, but the text commented upon is still visible as highlighted text. To view the comment, move the cursor over one of the highlights. A pop-up window appears with the reviewer's name and the text of the comment.

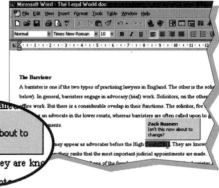

5 To see how comments appear when collaborating with other people, you must change the original user information stored within Word. Select Options from the Tools menu and under the User Information tab in the Options dialog box type in a new name and initials. Click the OK button.

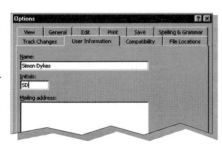

6 Insert another comment in your Word document and you'll see how Word differentiates between different commentators.

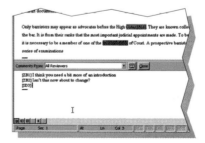

7 To view only one person's comments, use the drop-down list box on the dividing bar to select the appropriate name.

8 The other person's comments disappear from view, leaving you to focus on your selected commentator.

PC TIPS

Sound comments

The cassette button that appears on the dividing bar allows you to insert a sound recording as a comment. This works very much like inserting a sound recording in a document (see Stage 5, pages 22-23). An icon indicating a sound comment appears in the comments panel. Be aware, however, that sound files can be large and they increase the size of the document by a huge proportion. If you email them to colleagues, online costs will increase.

Using Word's Help

There is a long and curious tradition among computer users to refuse to seek help from the most obvious source – the Help menu of whatever program is currently open. Word's Help files offer particularly good advice.

Most Windows programs feature Help menus stuffed full of useful information just a mouse-click away. But it's often those who need help the most that are least likely to know where to find it. Others might feel that turning to a resource called Help is akin to an admission of defeat. This is a shame, because the Help files in Microsoft Word (and in many other programs) are full of comprehensive and useful advice.

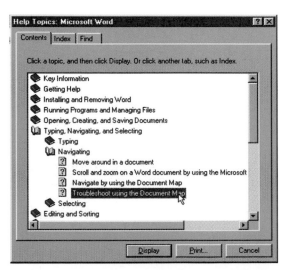

As software comes with increasingly less paper documentation, the Help file has become an essential part of the program. Help Topics in Word are both extensive and detailed.

● Help is at hand

As more and more programs are sold pre-installed on new computers, fewer and fewer are being shipped with full documentation. A thick printed manual is almost always the most expensive part of any software package and big companies can save millions of pounds by leaving them out. In such cases, the most immediate recourse is the program's built-in Help resource.

In Word, Help comes in various forms and, if you haven't explored it fully, you may be surprised at how much information is available. At its simplest, the Office Assistants, including characters such as Mr Clippit, have made great strides in introducing the Help resource. Many feel reluctant to ask advice of animated characters and it is therefore possible to customize the Office Assistants. You can also ignore them, or even turn them off altogether, and go straight to the Help Contents and Index pages if you prefer.

The friendly nature of Word's Help options shouldn't fool you into thinking that only beginners are catered for.

If Mr Clippit starts to annoy you, his appearance can easily be changed – see Office Assistants box, opposite.

Word's Help window has three sections, each with its own tab. The Contents section is a good place to get an overview of what Word has to offer. Double-click on the chapter you're interested in and select a subheading to find some general information about a topic. If your query is more specific, you can search the Help Index for individual words. The Help window also has a third tab called Find. This works in a similar way to the Index tab, but it is more powerful. For example, you can type in two words and it will then locate topics which mention both words. Often, using the Find tab yields more topic matches than the Index tab. You can click the Find tab's Options button if you want to modify the search. For instance, you can tell Word that you only want to see topics where both words appear in the order you typed them. This is particularly useful for locating a certain phrase. If you're using Word 97, the next source of help is the Microsoft on the Web

menu. This offers easy access to a host of useful information, downloadable files and online magazines. Log on to the Web, make your selection from the menu, and Word will automatically open up the page in your Web browser. This area of the site was created for the whole Microsoft Office suite of programs, so you'll also find information and files for other Microsoft programs such as Excel.

● **Online support**
The Online Support area plugs you into Microsoft's complete 'Knowledge Base' of techniques, problems, bugs and solutions. Just fill in the on-screen form to ask your question. This support resource can get very busy, so it might take a while to receive an answer.

The main area of Word-specific interest on the site is the Enhancements & Assistance area. The Enhancements page offers a list of downloadable files with added functionality. These include templates and an excellent Weblinks Help file, which adds hyperlinks in many Word Help topics to Microsoft's Web-based Knowledge Base articles.

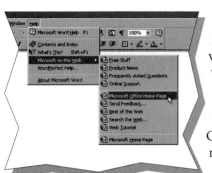

In Word 97, use the Help menu at the top of the Word screen to go to Microsoft on the Web. Go directly to the Office Home Page. There you can download the Office Assistants discussed in the box below. Word 2000 has similar links.

Office Assistants

If you appreciate the help Mr Clippit offers, but can't get along with the animated paper clip itself, why not change it?

LOVE THEM OR loathe them, the Microsoft Office Assistants do serve a vital purpose. Mr Clippit (the default Assistant) and the other animated characters Word has provided to make life easy for you, introduce the notion of Help and genuinely go some way to reassuring novices that computers are not intrinsically unfathomable by design.

You can customize your Assistant by double-clicking on it and clicking the Options button. For example, you might want to turn off sounds, specify that your Assistant moves aside automatically if it is in the way, or get it to take a guess at the Help topics.

If you become tired of your Office Assistant, there are two routes open to you. You can stop using it, in which case you might want to customize your Word toolbar to remove the Office Assistant Help and replace it (or complement it) with a Help Contents and Index button. Alternatively, you might want a new Assistant.

The number of Assistants available depends on which version of Word you have. To check, call up your Assistant, double-click on it, click Options, then the Gallery tab and click your way back and forth through the Assistants. Either select a different one or, if you don't see one you like, check out Microsoft's Web site http://office.microsoft.com/downloads/ which has a wide range of Assistants available for downloading. These include Kairu the Dolphin and F1 the Robot.

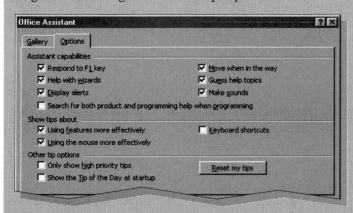

If you double-click on your Office Assistant and select Options, the screen shown on the left appears, allowing you to alter the way it behaves. Below are some of the different faces (Robot, Rocky and Dolphin) you can download via the Gallery tab.

Managing tax

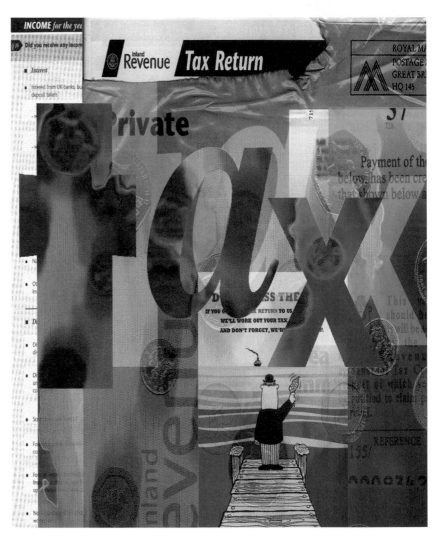

No one likes filling in forms and one of the least popular must be the annual tax return. Quicken can help you to set up your financial affairs so that preparing your tax return becomes a lot less stressful.

Using Quicken can make filling in a tax return and keeping track of tax deductible expenses much easier. You need to spend a little time preparing the software to suit your circumstances but this won't take long, and you only have to do it once.

The main task is to set up categories that enable Quicken to work out which transactions matter for tax. Quicken will not be able to do all the hard work for you unless you set up categories that correspond to the right tax brackets – and you enter all details of your expenditure and income in the right categories (see Stage 5, pages 84-87).

● Is it taxable?

Quicken's tax reporting features use the categories to sort and total different types of transaction. To get Quicken ready to handle tax, you need to assign each category to a second list that links different types of tax-related items. Quicken will use this second list to see which category should be reported in a tax summary. For example, if you enter a transaction to record the payment for cinema tickets, you would allocate it to the Entertainment category. As this is a personal expense, you do not have to assign the Entertainment category to a tax item.

In contrast, the interest you receive from bank or building society savings accounts should be entered in the Bank Interest category, and this category needs to be linked to the tax line: Building Society Interest – tax deducted.

● Setting up categories

Unfortunately, the only way of setting up Quicken so that each category is assigned to its correct tax line is by manually editing each category entry.

There are two different ways of doing this: by using the Tax Link Assistant or by using the Category List. The first is easier if you are

Quicken can help you keep all your financial affairs in line. Even the dreaded task of filling in your tax return is much less daunting with Quicken.

HELP!

The tax tracking features of Quicken help you to manage your affairs and quickly pull together all the transactions that need to be included on your tax return form. However, you will need to fill in the form, obtain your own tax advice, and calculate the tax you will have to pay. As with all tax matters, you should talk to your accountant or tax adviser to make sure that you have set up your software correctly, so that they can use the reports to help organize your tax.

Intuit™ Quicken®

SETTING UP QUICKEN TO TRACK TAX

Before Quicken can track your expenses for tax purposes, you need to make a vital change. First, select Options from the Edit menu and then select International from the sub-menu that appears. When the International Options dialog box appears, make sure that the Use Tax Return with Categories option box is ticked. Click on OK to complete the setup.

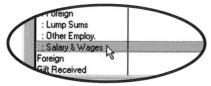

experienced with Quicken and tax-related terminology. The second is much easier for most other users and poses the least problems. On the following pages we show both methods, so you can choose the one you prefer to use.

● Taxable income examples

If you have savings held in a building society or bank savings account, you will probably be receiving interest on the money. This interest is a form of income and so needs to be declared on your tax return. For most savers, the tax due on the interest is automatically deducted by the bank or building society (these accounts pay net interest). Some accounts will pay interest gross of tax (that is, without deducting tax); these include those held by children, and people whose income is below the tax threshold.

Similarly, ISAs and other tax-free savings schemes will give you interest that must be declared. The tax office has to know about all your sources of income, even if you do not need to pay tax on the income. To make sure that all savings are reported, you should enter any interest you receive into the correct category and check your savings account to see if the money you have received is paid net or gross of tax; this will tell you which tax line to assign to the category. Many stocks and shares pay dividends to the shareholders

once a year as a form of bonus. This is also income and needs to be included on your tax return. When you pay your dividends into your bank account, make sure that you enter the correct category for the transaction, and then link this category to the correct tax line. Similarly, when you sell your shares you will need to make sure any capital gains are recorded appropriately for tax purposes (shares are covered on pages 62-65).

● Tax reports

Quicken has several different reports that use the information stored in your accounts to help prepare for your tax return. Remember that none of the reports will actually calculate the tax that you owe, but you can use the reports to prepare your financial affairs to give the data required on the tax return form or to enter into a tax calculation program. In this section, we look at the ways you can use the reports for your personal tax returns.

There are two main types of report, called Tax Summary and Tax Return. The Tax Summary provides a formatted report that displays every transaction that is in a qualifying category (for example, a category assigned to a tax item line). The Tax Return displays lots of detail, including all the separate parts of each transaction (such as tax and National Insurance deducted from your salary) and summarizes the totals.

Using the Tax Link Assistant

Quicken has two ways of assigning transaction categories to different tax lines. Here we show how to use Quicken's built-in assistance to help you decide.

1 Select Taxes from the Features menu and then the Set Up for Taxes option from the Taxes sub-menu.

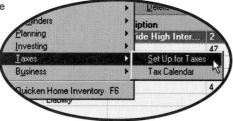

2 The Tax Link Assistant window opens. On the left is a list of current Categories and on the right are the separate tax line items.

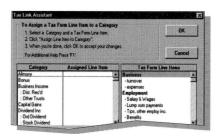

3 Start by telling Quicken that your salary should be grouped under the Salary line for tax purposes: click on the Salary & Wages Category on the left. Your selection is highlighted.

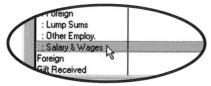

4 Now scroll through the list on the right to find the correct tax line. In this case it has the same name, but for other categories it will be different. Click on the Salary & Wages item.

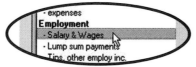

5 To link the two items, click the Assign Line Item to Category button. You need to repeat this process for each type of transaction that has tax implications.

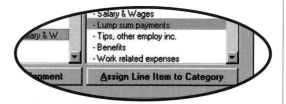

Categories and tax lines

The first step in managing your taxes with Quicken is to set up each category so that it is assigned to the correct tax item – otherwise you might find that your share income, for example, is taxed as current earnings or your petrol treated as capital expenditure.

1 To set up your income and expenditure categories, select the Lists menu and choose the Category/Transfer option.

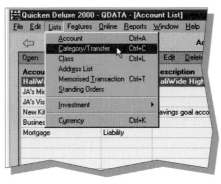

2 The main screen now changes to display all the categories that Quicken currently has stored. Some categories, such as Car, have sub-categories, such as service and petrol. This main list displays all categories including income and expenses.

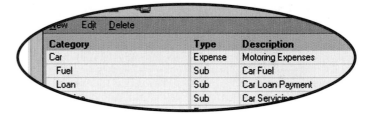

3 Start by setting up your income categories to define how each is analysed for tax. Click on the Options button and then select the Display Income Categories command.

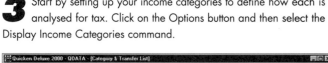

4 Start with the category used to record interest from building society accounts. Scroll down the list and click on the Bank Interest sub-category just below the Interest Inc category.

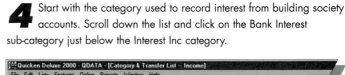

5 Now click the Edit button at the top left corner of the screen to bring up all the category details.

6 The category's information window appears. At the bottom of the window is the tax information. If you cannot see this, you need to configure Quicken to support tax (see Setting up Quicken to track tax, see page 53).

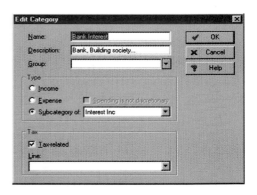

7 Click on the Line drop-down list box in the Tax section to see the various tax lines available. Most building society and bank accounts have tax deducted by the society, so select the item: Banks, build society, etc: Interest after tax deducted. Click the OK button to link the category to this tax line.

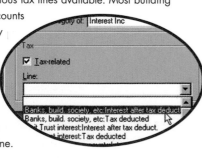

8 You now need to follow the same process to cover each type of transaction that has tax implications – both income and expenses. It's a repetitive process, but you'll only need to do it once.

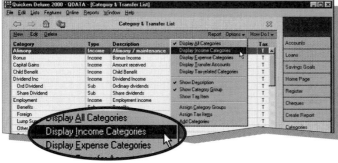

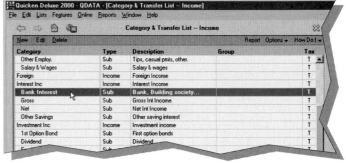

Using Quicken's tax-related reports

Quicken can produce a concise summary of your tax affairs quickly and easily. Here we show you how to use the Tax Summary features.

PC TIPS

Choosing information

You don't have to include all the pieces of information for tax-related transactions listed in the Tax Summary. Use the Show Columns section of the Customise Tax Summary Report dialog box to turn off items of information you don't want to see on the report. Do this by removing the tick next to the relevant column.

1 Click on the Banking command in the Reports menu and select the Tax Return option from the sub-menu.

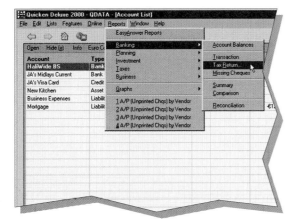

2 The Create Report screen appears, listing the types of report available. Click on the Tax Summary report. (The other tabs cover reports for tracking investments and for business users.)

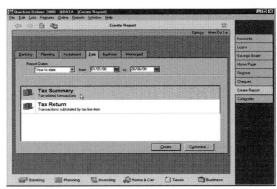

3 In the UK, the tax year runs from 6 April through to the following 5 April, so to see the summary for the most recently completed tax year, type these appropriate dates into the 'from' and 'to' date boxes.

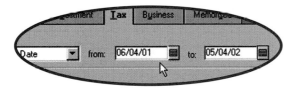

4 To specify the way you want all this information to be presented in the report for the tax return, click on the Customise button near the bottom of the screen.

5 In the dialog box that appears, select Tax Return in the Subtotal By box. This will ensure that only those transactions allocated to the tax-related categories you specifically set up (as shown on the previous page) are included in the final report.

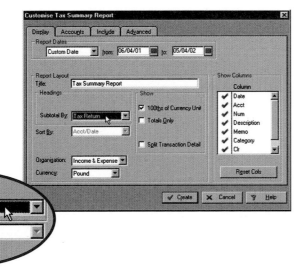

6 Click on the Create button to display the report. The window shows the formatted report with your tax-related income and your tax-related expenses.

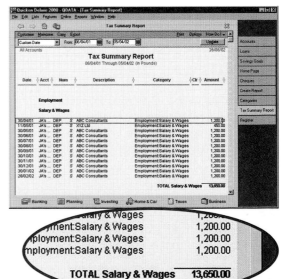

Balancing your budget

There are plenty of handy tools provided with Quicken. Among the most useful are the budget-planning features. These can help ensure that you are always in control of your finances.

There are several tools provided by Quicken to help you manage your budgets. The first step, however, is to create the budget plan, and the best way of doing this is to focus on just one or two categories. We will use Groceries and Household and monitor these each month.

Before you start, you need to give Quicken an idea of the amounts you expect to spend on these categories. You can work out an estimate and set your month-by-month spending plans with Quicken's planning tool (see Stage 6, pages 56-57). Better still, you can let Quicken analyse the historical information that you've already entered and produce a basic budget for you. Your budget plan will provide the key foundation for your spending each month. If you want to keep closer control over any particular individual categories, such as cash spending, eating out or entertainment, you could enter budget amounts for each, covering a two-week period.

You can use Quicken's Progress Bars to see quickly and clearly if you are managing to stay within your budgets. Under the Features menu, select Planning and you will find the Progress Bars option.

For expenses that do not occur as often, such as electricity, water or other utility bills, you might find a quarterly or yearly budget easier to manage.

● Reporting features
With the budget information entered, you can use Quicken's reporting features to monitor your real spending against your planned budget. It's best if you try to run a basic report on a regular basis to monitor the way in which your spending matches the original budget plan.

Another way to monitor your spending is to use Quicken's Progress Bar feature. This will display an instant view of how your finances are matching your planned budget.

● Planning your savings
You can just as easily use the budgeting feature to help you plan your savings. Use the same techniques we look at here to plan for and monitor a category assigned to your savings. By using the budget function, you will be able to exercise better control over all your finances – savings and spending alike.

It's easy for family finances to get on top of you, but with Quicken you have a powerful friend on your side.

Creating a spending budget

Quicken will help you monitor how well you are staying on budget.

1 Select the Budget My Spending option from the menu that appears when the mouse is over Quicken's Planning icon.

2 If this is your first budget, click OK when the First Time in Budgets dialog box appears. When the Budget screen appears, click the Edit button and select Clear All.

3 Click the Yes button to confirm your action, then click the Edit button and select Autocreate.

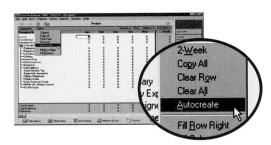

4 Now enter the dates Quicken will use as the basis for creating a budget from your previous transactions. Type the dates into the two boxes in the Transactions section, making sure the Use Monthly Detail option is selected. Click on the Categories button.

5 A large dialog box listing all of Quicken's categories appears. Select the lines you want to monitor. In this case, we only want to cover Clothing and Entertainment. The quickest way to specify these is to click the Clear All button and then scroll through the list, clicking on those categories you want to place a tick next to. Click the OK button to return to the Budget screen.

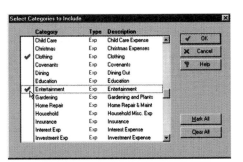

PC TIPS

To regulate your spending each month, select the Use Average for Period option in Step 4. Quicken calculates an average for transactions over the period and enters these into the budget.

6 The full listing looks daunting. To hide all the zeros, click the Categories button and then click the Clear 0 Amounts button. Click the OK button. To limit the display to the categories you selected, click the View button and choose Zero Budget Categories from the menu.

7 The display now shows budget figures based on your past spending. If you want to change any of the figures, click on them and type a new amount.

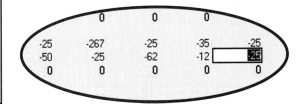

8 As you enter real transactions for these categories, you can create reports to compare actual spending and budget. Click on the Reports menu, choose the Planning option and select Monthly Budget from the sub-menu. When the Create Report screen appears, click the Create button.

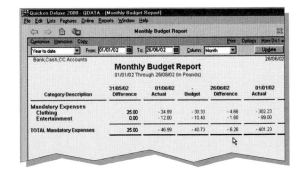

9 When the report appears on-screen, you can clearly see how you are performing financially in relation to your planned budget. The numbers in red in the Difference columns show where you've gone astray.

Household reports

Quicken is great at managing your financial affairs and, in addition, its powerful features can help organize other elements of your home life.

Although most of the dozens of different types of reports available within Quicken are designed to help you manage your financial life more effectively, the program also includes features that assist you in organizing other domestic affairs that don't involve accounting.

These help you manage the home, insurance and personal records you might need to find quickly in an emergency.

● List your possessions

One useful report helps you to regulate your home insurance by recording the appropriate details about all the valuable items that you own, such as TV and video recorder.

This inventory feature lets you enter details of all the valuables in your house, room by room. Once you have entered this information, you can use Quicken to check that your current home-contents insurance is adequate and the inventory also provides a crucial record in case of an accident, a fire or a burglary. In such a situation, a comprehensive list of your possessions is an invaluable aid to help you discover what's been stolen or damaged.

In addition to storing details on your home contents within the Home Inventory database, you can also record details of your insurance policies, such as insurance company, policy number and any agent's details. Keeping all of this information together means that it is quick and easy to retrieve the details should you ever need to make a claim.

● Help making a claim

In the unfortunate event of any kind of incident that causes loss or damage, a written insurance claim will probably be necessary. So having a home inventory report means that you have details to hand for the insurance claim. Quicken makes the construction of the report easy. Possessions are listed by location in the home: living room, kitchen, garage, for example. They are then sub-divided into categories such as furnishings or electronic equipment. This sub-division helps ensure that you don't leave out any possessions.

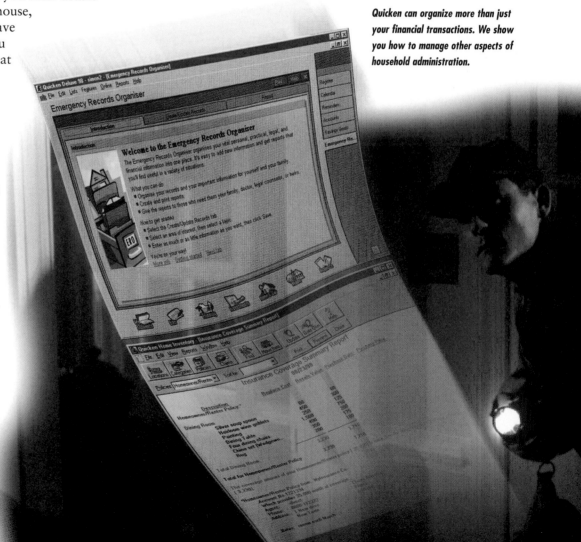

Quicken can organize more than just your financial transactions. We show you how to manage other aspects of household administration.

Intuit™ Quicken®

Printing

If your home is burgled and your computer is stolen, then you're in trouble unless you have kept a printout of your records.

If you are using either the Home Insurance or Emergency Record feature of Quicken, make sure that once you have entered all the details, you print out a hard copy of the information. Use the Print button near the top right of each report window to produce a formatted copy that you can keep on file.

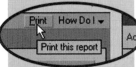

Similarly, a fire might destroy your computer. It is a good idea to keep your report printouts in a fireproof place. Or alternatively, you might ask a relation or a friend to store a copy, just in case.

Each item can be given a current, resale and a replacement value. Quicken will automatically total up the values so that you can find out how much home-contents insurance cover you need to purchase and if you are under- or over-insured.

● In an emergency

In case an emergency should ever arise, you should ensure that you have a file with all your important information written down. You can use Quicken's Emergency Records feature to store the contact details of your local doctor, your relatives and insurance and medical information. It helps you to gather together these vital records into one, handy location.

Most people store all their household paperwork and information in categories. For example, all your mortgage information will be in one file, your car insurance and other motoring documents somewhere else, and details of guarantees for your electrical equipment in another place. This can work well as a filing system if you are organized and tidy, but it makes finding important details from each file a long process. By using the Emergency Records feature, you can enter the most important information from each

BACKING UP QUICKEN DATA

Often, it's only when you start typing your family's personal data into Quicken's Emergency Records Organizer that you realize the sheer volume of information that you are collating. However, you need to bear in mind that your Quicken financial data and your transactions quickly build up into a significant volume of work over time. Even if you hardly ever back up letters and other documents, retyping just a few month's Quicken transactions would take ages.

From time to time, Quicken prompts you and asks if you want to create a backup file. Think of this prompt as a useful reminder and click the Backup button when you see the Automatic Backup dialog box. You can also back up at any time by selecting Backup from the File menu.

category into Quicken: your insurance policy number and contact details for your car, home and life insurance; the details from your working life including your National Insurance number, tax office and so on. Then whenever you need to find the information, you can turn to Quicken, rather than trawling through your personal filing system.

Quick and easy report creation

Here we show you that the quickest and easiest way of creating reports is also often the most useful, as it avoids any complex accounting terminology.

IF YOU WANT to keep tighter control over your money, you can use the wide range of Quicken financial reports to help you understand how you spend every pound. However, many of the reports use complex accounting terms that can be confusing. To solve this, Quicken includes EasyAnswer reports that are listed under questions you might want to ask, for example: 'How much am I worth?', 'How is my investment performing?', and so on.

If you know what you want to ask, but you're not sure of the technical accounting term to describe this, start with an EasyAnswer report. Once you are more experienced with Quicken and organizing your finances, you can use the custom reports to provide more specific answers. Custom reports provide more detail and can be tailored to analyse any part of your finances.

There are specific reports that do not cover finances, but are important in other areas. These reports include insurance valuations, records of family members, doctors and so on – all the details that are essential to have in the event of a crisis.

You can access the EasyAnswer reports from the Reports menu option (right) or use the Report on my income and expenses option from the Banking icon at the bottom left of the main Quicken window (below).

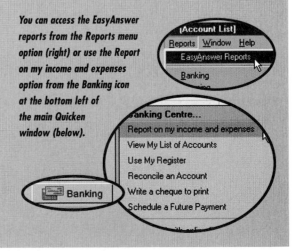

Setting up an Emergency Records report

During a crisis, it is essential to have easy access to household records. Quicken can save you from rummaging through your paper files by ensuring you have information to hand.

1 Select the Home & Car icon at the bottom of the Quicken screen and choose the Organise emergency records option.

2 You now see the introduction screen to the emergency planning section. Read through the introduction to see how this feature works. Then click on the middle tab at the top of the window, labelled Create/Update Records.

3 There are three main sections to this screen, numbered 1–3. First, move to the top left-hand corner to select the area of your emergency records that you want to create. Click on the drop-down list. The Adults' Important Info area from the list is an excellent starting point.

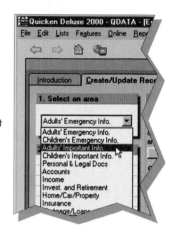

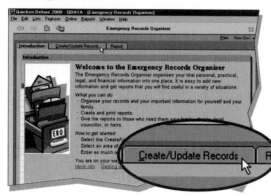

4 Now you have chosen an area, you need to select the specific topic within this area. The part of the screen labelled 2 contains the topics for this area. Start by selecting the Summary option.

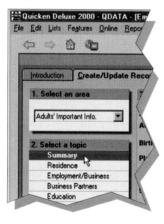

5 Now move to the main part of the screen, section 3, to enter the information for this topic. Type in the name, address and personal details of the adult members of your family.

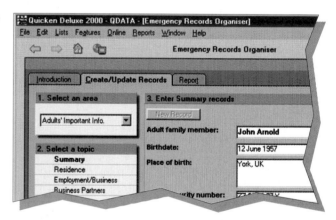

6 Click on the Save button at the bottom of the screen to store this information. Change to Adults' Emergency Info in the area selection and choose Doctors/Dentists in the Select a topic section; enter the details of your doctor and dentist in the main window on the right of the screen. Click Save again to store this information.

7 Now you can create a report that lists the information stored in the emergency records. Click on the Report tab at the top of the window. Choose Emergency Report from the drop-down list at the top of the new screen.

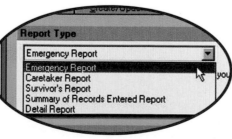

8 At the bottom of the window is the information that would be required in the event of an emergency. It includes contact details of members of the family, doctors and relatives. You can use the scroll bar on the right-hand side of the window to view the rest of the report.

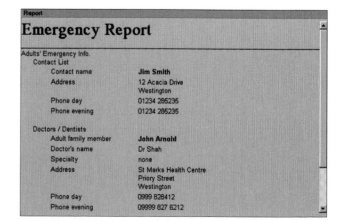

Producing an insurance coverage report

Here we use Quicken to create a report that could save you money now and worry later. It tells you whether you are over- or under-insured.

1 Place your mouse pointer over the Home & Car icon at the bottom of the screen and choose the Record My Home Inventory menu option. Click the Continue button when the Welcome dialog box appears.

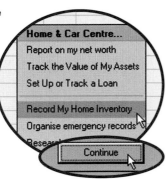

2 The special Home Inventory program starts and displays columns that allow you to enter the description and value of your items, arranged by room or location.

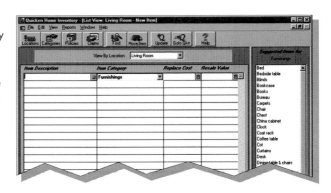

3 Start by entering the valuables in your dining room. Click on the drop-down View By Location list near the top of the screen and select Dining Room from the list.

4 Click on the cell in the top left-hand corner of the grid displayed in the main part of the screen. The first column stores the description of each item. Start entering your valuable items.

5 Move your mouse pointer to the second column and click on the drop-down list box that provides all the categories for your items. Select the Jewellery & Valuables option for the silver spoon.

6 Now enter £80 as the replacement cost of the spoon in the third column. Quicken fills in the resale value with half the value of the replacement cost. Change this to a more realistic £60 resale value.

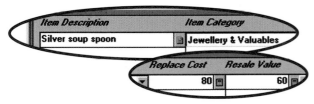

7 To enter the details of the insurance policy, click on the Policies button at the top of the screen. Quicken displays a list of all your possible policies; select the Homeowner/Renter policy to highlight the line and click on the Edit button.

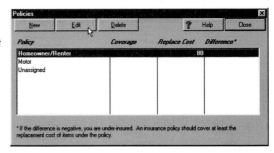

8 Enter the home insurance policy details, including the total value insured, policy number and contact details. Click on OK to save the details and return to the Policies window.

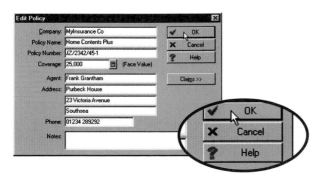

9 Close the Policies window and repeat Steps 3 to 7 for each item in your home. Then choose the Insurance Coverage Summary option from the Reports drop-down menu. You can see the insured goods in each room and the comparison of total replacement cost with your insurance coverage.

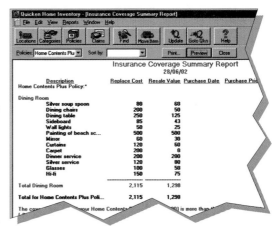

Managing your investments

Quicken has features that can help you manage investments, such as stocks and shares. You can do this manually or make use of the information that is provided by Quicken's online Internet service.

If you hold a selection of stocks or shares (which Quicken calls securities), it's easy to group them together within an electronic investment portfolio and use Quicken to record the transactions whenever you buy and sell. You can also use the program to help maximize your profits and to manage your capital gains tax declaration at the end of each financial year.

If you are used to looking in a newspaper to check the value of your shares, Quicken can make this far easier. You will need an Internet account to access Quicken's online feature (see Setting up Quicken online box, below) but once connected, the program will automatically display up-to-date share data. You can get a valuation on your current share holdings, view general trading data or keep a record of historical prices, building up a profile to help you decide when to buy or sell.

Users who don't have an Internet account can still use Quicken to monitor shares and track prices by entering newspaper share price information manually. The best way to do this is to enter the data on a particular day each week, and keep to a regular pattern to build a picture of share changes over time.

● Online share valuation

The simplest way to use the online service is to do an instant check on the current share price. This uses Quicken as a Web browser in order to display the Quicken Web site automatically. From this Web page you can display the latest prices of any share, as well as extra information, such as the volume of shares traded during the day.

● Trading data

Together with the spot-checks on share prices, the Quicken Web site delivers a summary of information about almost every type of security traded on the main stock exchanges. This feature is not automatic, but you need only to enter the share's special code (see Finding share symbols, opposite) to view the price highs and lows for a company.

It's easy to monitor the value of stocks and shares by entering them from newspaper listings, or by accessing the up-to-date trading data supplied on Quicken's own Web site.

SETTING UP QUICKEN ONLINE

Quicken's online features all use the Quicken Web site, which provides financial news, share prices and background information. To make use of the online feature, you will need a modem connected to your computer and an account with an Internet service provider (ISP).

Whenever Quicken is running, you can then use it to connect to the Internet and access the Quicken site automatically. All you need to do is to choose the Online menu option.

If you are not running the Quicken software, you can still access the Web site by using a standard browser, such as Netscape Navigator or Internet Explorer (although you will not be able to update your share information automatically). Just enter the Web site address (www.quicken.co.uk).

● Spotting trends

Quicken's online data provides the same sort of service as a newspaper, but is more up to date. However, to use the power of Quicken fully, you should record share price information regularly. You can then build up a record of a company's share price changes.

There's no need to buy the shares, as you can simply ask the program to monitor their valuation. Once you have set this up, you can then download the latest prices automatically and store them in a historical data file. If you update this at the end of each day, you'll soon build up an accurate picture of the share price movements. The information can be displayed in graph form to show trends in these movements.

Using Quicken's share tracking and price graphing functions, you will find it easier to spot when a given company's shares are moving consistently up or down. The graph can be viewed on screen or printed out to find the best times to buy and sell your shares. Quicken does not offer any advice, but there is analysis software available to help you decide when it would be prudent to trade.

Finding share symbols

Stock exchanges use short text symbols as a form of financial shorthand for the company's full name. You can look them up from within Quicken.

1 If you don't know the symbol for a share you're interested in, bring up the Set Up Security dialog box as shown in Step 4 on page 64. Type the first part of the name of the security into the Name box and click the Look up button.

2 Quicken opens your Web browser and connects to the Internet. It uses the financial section of the Excite Web site to search for securities that match the name you entered. In this case there are many 'Halifax' securities, but none are the one we want. Click the Next Page link.

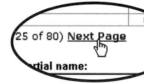

3 Keep looking until you find the right share. In this case, it's the Halifax Group, which the site tells us has the symbol HFX.

4 Select the symbol and right-click on it. Select Copy from the pop-up menu.

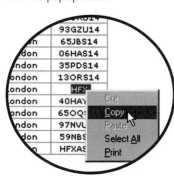

5 Now click the Go back to Quicken button on the small floating window to return to the Set Up Security dialog box.

6 Click on the Symbol box and press [Ctrl]+[V] to paste the symbol you copied in Step 4. Now you can continue setting up your information.

How to monitor a share price

Before you can monitor the price of particular shares over time, you need to add them to Quicken's Security List and set them up in your personal investment portfolio.

1 Select the Lists menu and choose the Investment option. From the sub-menu, choose the Security option.

2 Quicken displays its Security List. If you already have a portfolio, information about the shares will be listed here. As we haven't entered any data yet, the list is blank.

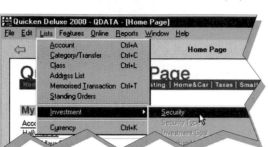

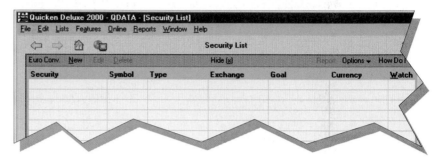

3 To add a new share (which Quicken calls a new security), click on the New button in the top left-hand corner of the window.

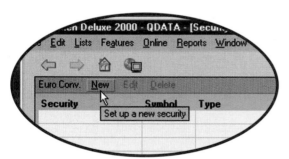

4 You can now enter the basic information about the share that you want to monitor. Type in the name of the share, Alliance & Leicester. Move to the Symbol box and enter the unique code for this share; you can use the Look up button if you don't know the symbol for your share (see Finding share symbols on page 63). You can also change the currency in which the price is displayed – we are keeping the default, which is in pounds sterling – by clicking on the arrow and selecting the required currency from the list.

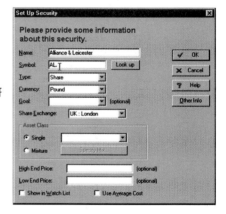

5 To tell Quicken that we only want to monitor these shares and not to buy any, check the Show in Watch List option. Click on the OK button to save the set-up data.

6 To view the share data, we need to open our personal investment portfolio. Move the pointer over the Investing icon at the bottom of the screen and choose the View My Portfolio option.

7 Now the Portfolio View shows the data about shares that we are monitoring but haven't bought. If you cannot see your share, select Watch List from the Group by box. You're now ready to update share values (see opposite).

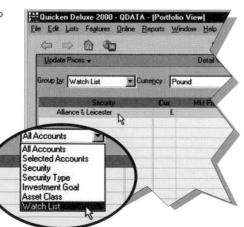

Updating share data

Once you have set up a share in your personal investment portfolio, you can access Quicken's
Web site and update the data as often as you want, via your Internet account and modem.
Here, we update the Alliance & Leicester shares we added to our portfolio on page 64.

1 Start by displaying the
share data in your
portfolio, as shown on
the previous page.
Now click on the
Update Prices button
in the top left-hand
corner of the window
and choose the Get
Online Quotes option.

2 Quicken
displays a
dialog box which tells
you that it will connect
to the Internet to
download share
prices. Click on the
Update Now button
to continue.

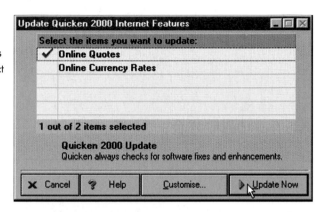

3 The update process is automatic. Quicken
displays a status window that shows you how
the operation is progressing.

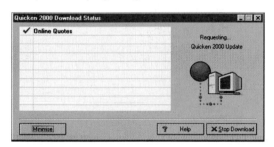

4 Once Quicken has
downloaded the
current data, it tells you
that it has finished and
displays a summary of the
updates that the program
has made. Click on the
Done button to continue.

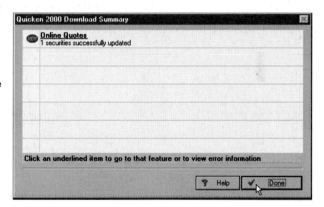

5 This takes you back to the Portfolio View
screen. Now click on the Detail View button at
the top of the window, near the centre. This tells
Quicken to display more detail about the Alliance
& Leicester shares.

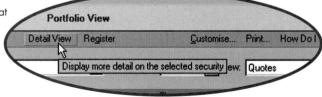

6 The Security Detail View window
displays four main panels of
information. The one at top left shows how
many shares you own and lists any profit
or loss. The one at top right shows share
transactions. (Neither of these panels
applies to shares that you are only
monitoring.) The graphic displays in the
bottom half of the window show the
historical volume of sales and the
up-and-down movement of the share price
over the period you are monitoring.

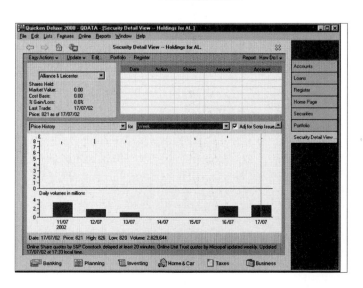

PC TIPS

Manual data entries

If you do not have
access to the Internet,
you can add share
prices to Quicken
from the listing in a
newspaper. In the
Portfolio View, all
you have to do is
type the value into
the Mkt Price column.
To record past prices,
change the date in
the Portfolio as of
box in the Portfolio
View. You can
also enter share
movement and
volume information
in the appropriate
columns.

Using non-text frames

Frames can be used to contain non-text as well as text elements on a page. Here we look at how to use frames designed for holding graphics and tables.

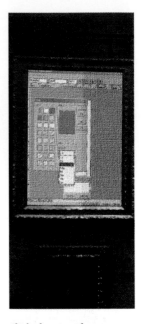

Think of non-text frames as containers that hold the pictorial elements on a page and make it easy to move or resize them. The frames themselves can be invisible, or you can give them their own decorative borders.

When using Publisher, all the different text elements you want to include on a page have to be placed in what the program calls 'frames'. These are simply containers that make it easy to position individual components of your work (see Stage 6, pages 82-85).

Non-text elements, such as graphics, also have their own frames that work in almost exactly the same way. There are different types of frame to hold tables, WordArt (logos and other text with decorative effects), pictures and ready-to-use clip-art images from Publisher's Clip Gallery. The usual procedure is to select the appropriate frame tool (see Adding non-text frame tools box, opposite), draw a box and add the contents.

Each frame (and its contents) can then be moved round and placed in an exact position on the page, aligning it precisely against guide marks and ruler lines. You can move frames from one page to another and you can copy them to somewhere else in a document. If you are not sure whether to include certain frames on your page, you can store frames and their contents temporarily on the pasteboard area around each page.

● **Table frames**

The first non-text frame tool option is used for inserting Publisher tables. These tables are ideal if you have words and figures to organize into rows and columns.

When you click on the Table Frame Tool, you see a grid that looks like a spreadsheet. You can put information into the grid either by typing directly into one of the cells, inserting some data via the Insert menu, or by cutting and pasting from another document. If that document is an Excel spreadsheet, you can copy whole rows and columns directly into a Publisher table.

The Table Frame Tool's most obvious use is for something like a price list or a financial statement, with one column of text (items for sale or budgetary headings) alongside one of numbers (quantities, prices, financial data). But Publisher's tables can also be used for other purposes. A contents panel in a newsletter, for instance, is basically one column of text, such as chapter headings or article titles, alongside another column of page numbers.

MIXING FRAMES

In general, you can't put one Publisher frame inside another. So if you want to include a picture as, say, part of a table of contents, it isn't possible to place a picture frame within a table frame. You solve this problem by placing one frame on top of another, building them up in transparent layers. For example, you can put a picture frame on top of the table frame, making both equal in size.

● WordArt frames

The next frame tool is for WordArt. This is Publisher's tool for special text effects, which you can use to create logos, eye-catching messages, impressive headlines and so on (see Stage 1, pages 44-45).

You can use any of the available typefaces and choose any type size as you do when working with ordinary text. You can also use any of the usual paragraph alignment options (right or left justified, or centred). Unlike ordinary text, however, WordArt can be bent, curved and twisted into any shape. The graphic effects available also go well beyond simply selecting a colour. You can apply a pattern to the text and choose a second colour for a background. You can opt for a variety of shadow effects and you can even choose the shadow's colour.

WordArt isn't designed for handling large amounts of text, however. And you can't check the spelling in a WordArt frame, so you'll have to use a dictionary.

● Pictures and clip art

The two graphics frame tools let you draw boxes into which you can put any kind of image. The Picture Frame Tool is used to hold a picture that you have stored on disk, import an image using a scanner or copy an image from another document or program.

If you want an image from Publisher's Clip Gallery, there is a separate frame tool. This gives you instant access to the ready-to-go clip art, with the Clip Gallery popping up as soon as you have drawn the frame. However, apart from this, there is no real difference between a picture frame and a clip-art frame.

● Sizing pictures

Whatever type of image you import into a frame, Publisher keeps its original proportions, so when an image is loaded, it won't always fit in your box neatly. However, it's easy to alter both the height and width of any frame.

The simple option in such cases is to keep to the proportions of the original image and increase or decrease them to fit the size of the frame. Also, you can adjust the image to fit your frame by stretching or compressing it, which might work with clip art, but is unlikely to look very good for photographs. The other option is to 'crop' the image, trimming parts of it so that what's left will fit the proportions of your frame (see pages 70-71).

It's easy to use WordArt within a Publisher Wizard, such as the Masthead Creation Wizard used to create effective page headings.

Adding non-text frame tools

All the non-text frame tools are located in a tool bar on the left side of the main Publisher window, below the Text Frame Tool. They all operate in a similar way.

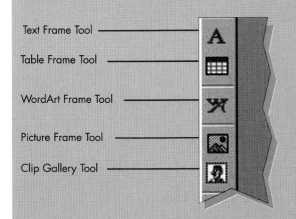

Text Frame Tool ——— A

Table Frame Tool ———

WordArt Frame Tool ———

Picture Frame Tool ———

Clip Gallery Tool ———

To use any of the frame tools, simply click on the appropriate button on the toolbar (left) and then move the mouse pointer across to the Publisher's document area.

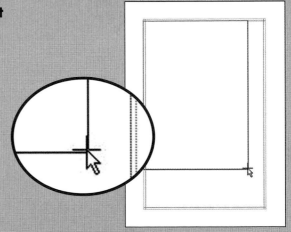

Once your mouse pointer is over the page, it will change to a crosshair (inset). Move this to where you want the top left of the frame to appear and hold down the left mouse button. Drag the mouse down and right to make the frame. Release the button when the frame is drawn.

Using a WordArt frame

WordArt frames let you create sophisticated text-based graphics. Here, we show you how to produce a birthday party invitation.

1 Open the Catalog (click File, then New if it isn't already in view). Go to Blank Publications and select Full Page. Click Create.

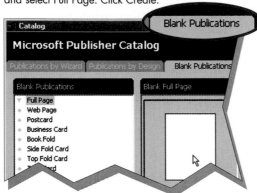

2 Click on the WordArt Frame Tool button. Move the cursor over to the page – it will change from an arrow into a crosshair – and place it on the top left corner of the margin guides. Hold down the left mouse button and drag down towards the bottom right to draw the frame. Release the button.

3 The WordArt window containing the words Your Text Here pops up. The Publisher screen changes to show the WordArt commands. Type your own message in the WordArt window that says Enter Your Text Here.

4 Click the typeface selector button and scroll down to find a suitable font. The changes will be reflected immediately in the WordArt frame.

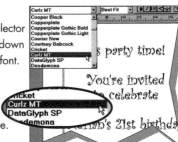

5 Click on the Text Effects box on the toolbar and select one of the options from the drop-down panel (inset). The changes will take place immediately, so you can view a few alternatives. Here we've applied an effect that runs the top and bottom text around two semi-circles.

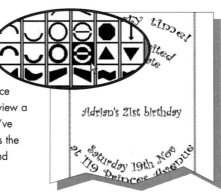

6 To select a colour for the text, click on the Shading button on the toolbar and then choose a Foreground colour.

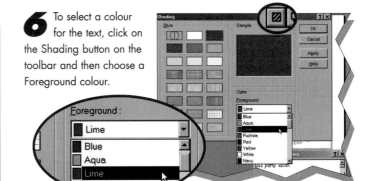

7 To give emphasis to the text, click on the Shadow button on the toolbar (inset) and select a shadow style from the row of examples shown as capital As. Now select a colour for the shadow from the drop-down list.

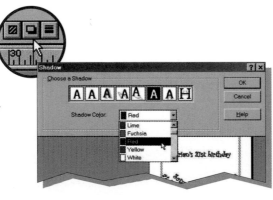

8 When you are happy with the results, click anywhere outside the WordArt frame to return to the main Publisher display, then save your work.

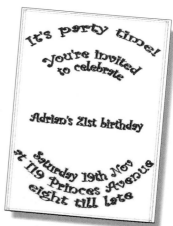

Combining frames

We'll use different types of frames for all the elements of a Christmas newsletter, including headline, text and pictures.

1 Start a new blank publication. Click on the WordArt Frame Tool and draw a frame for the newsletter title. Type in the text and format it in a similar way to that shown on the previous page.

2 Now we can add some main text. First, draw a text frame that occupies the rest of the page (see Stage 6, pages 82-85) and then use the Insert menu's Text File command to find some suitable text for inserting into the frame.

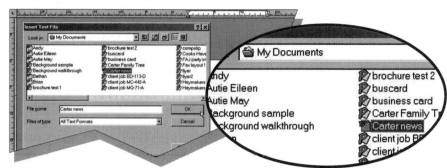

3 We'll brighten up the page with an image from Publisher's clip-art selection. Click on the Clip Gallery Tool and draw a frame on the page under the headline by holding down the left mouse button and dragging down and right.

4 When you release the mouse button, the Clip Gallery will pop up. Select the clip art you want and Publisher will place it in the frame (you might be asked to insert the Publisher CD). If the clip art does not fit exactly into the frame you have drawn, you can either keep to its original dimensions or drag on the edges to resize the image.

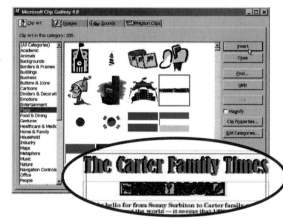

5 To insert a picture, such as a photo, click on the Picture Frame Tool and draw a box on the page to hold the image.

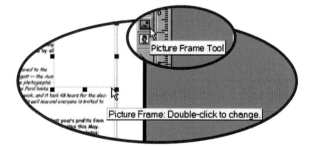

6 Double-click in the frame. The Insert Picture window will pop up. Locate the image you want to include – you can check it by clicking on the file name once to see a preview – and select it. Click the Insert button.

7 The picture will be inserted into the frame. As with clip art, its original dimensions might not fit exactly into the box you have drawn for it – but as photos look odd if you change their shape, it is better to keep to the original dimensions. Move the box to its final position on the page and save the finished job.

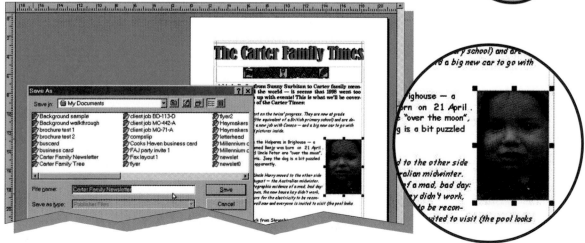

Using picture frames

You can add simple graphic shapes, such as boxes, circles and stars, to a document by using the drawing tools. But if you want more complicated graphics, you need a picture frame.

We have already seen how you can use either the Clip Gallery Tool or the Picture Frame Tool to import an image (see page 69). The difference is that the Clip Gallery Tool takes you to the Clip Gallery to select a graphic, while the Picture Frame Tool draws a frame to hold a picture that you then insert as a separate operation.

If you draw the frame first, Publisher will automatically size the picture you import to fit into the area as best it can. This might mean that the image won't necessarily fill the whole frame that you've drawn. Alternatively, you can bypass the frame-drawing by using the Insert menu and selecting Picture. This way, the graphic that you select will be imported in its original size and shape. Publisher draws the picture frame for you, and you can move and resize it later, which you might find a better option in some cases.

● Resizing a picture

Once you have a picture in your document, you can move it in the usual way by dragging the frame. You can also resize it by clicking on one of the edge markers and dragging it into a new shape. Use one of the corner handles if you want to maintain the frame's proportions, so that the width and height are automatically adjusted at the same time.

You can also resize a picture by using the Scale Picture command. Select the picture, click on the Format menu and choose Scale Picture. Specify the height and width as a percentage of the original size. If you enter the same percentage in each box, you'll get an exact, in-proportion copy of the original. If the percentages are different, this will result in a stretched version although, particularly with clip-art images, the distortion could be so small that it's unnoticeable.

● Composing a picture

There are two other things you can do using picture frames. First, you can add a border in exactly the same way as for any other frame (see pages 76-79). Second, you can 'crop' the picture, slicing unwanted areas off one or more edges to improve the composition of the remaining image, for example, getting rid of a boring background around a portrait. This doesn't physically remove anything – it just hides parts of the picture, so if you change your mind you can easily restore any of the cropped areas.

Picture frames are there to hold your graphics and can be used to resize and crop images.

PC TIPS

Margins

Usually, a picture fills the whole frame and if you add a border it will butt up against the edges of the image. But you can put a margin around a picture by leaving a gap between the image and the edge of the frame. To set the width of the margins, select Picture Frame Properties from the Format menu.

Margins	
Left	0.8 cm
Right	0.8 cm
Top	0.8 cm
Bottom	0.8 cm

Tweaking pictures

To see what you can do using picture frames, we're going to improve a family snapshot by cropping it.

PC TIPS

When you crop a picture, you click on a frame handle and drag it to select an area to cut out. If you hold down the [Ctrl] key while doing this, Publisher will automatically crop the same amount from the opposite side as well, keeping the centre of the picture in the middle of the frame.

1 Set up a blank document, go to the Insert menu and select Picture. Import any suitable image – Publisher will draw a picture frame to fit. Click on the picture to select it.

2 Before adjusting the size of the image, you have to go to the Format menu and click on Crop Picture.

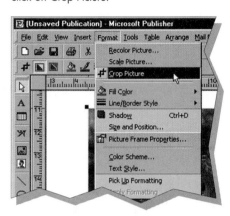

3 Position the cursor on the corner of the image where you want to start 'cutting'. When the cursor changes to the crop cursor, drag it across the picture. You'll see guidelines appear. The part of the picture to be removed is the L-shaped area over which you're moving the cursor – the rectangular shape is what you'll be left with.

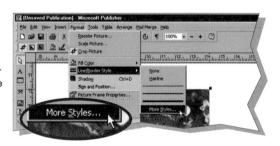

4 Don't worry if you get the cropping wrong – you can always use the Undo option on the Edit menu to restore the image to its original uncropped shape. When you have cropped the picture to the shape you want, click on Format. Select Line/Border Style and then More Styles.

5 Click on the BorderArt tab. Find a border for the picture, adjust the colours if you want to, and click OK.

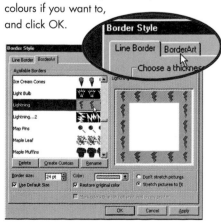

6 If you are happy with the result, save your work.

IMPORTING IMAGES

You can find graphic images for use in your publications from several different sources:

● Use Publisher's drawing tools for simple shapes like boxes and ovals. There's also a Custom Shapes tool for slightly more complicated designs such as stars and speech bubbles.

● Publisher comes with a good collection of ready-to-use photographs, images and fancy design objects on the CD. Other programs on your PC could well have similar collections of graphics that you can use.

● You can use a program such as Paint Shop Pro or Windows Paint to produce an image that you can then save on disk for later use.

● Photographs, prints or drawings can be scanned in, and then saved on disk.

● You can take a conventional reel of film to a photo lab and have your photos 'printed' as PhotoCD files. This will cost rather more than ordinary processing but you'll get a very high-resolution image on CD-ROM.

● A digital camera takes photos and stores them in its internal memory. When you want to use the pictures you can download them onto your PC. They are saved as individual graphics files, just like any other image. Digital cameras are still quite expensive, but bear in mind that you'll never need to buy film or pay for its processing.

Setting up tables

With its Table Frame Tool, Publisher can easily present data organized in a table comprising rows and columns. This tabular data might include month-by-month financial information, to-do lists, rotas, a contents table and even indented lists.

There is plenty of scope for a wide variety of tables within Publisher because the software lets you create tables as large as 128 columns by 128 rows. You can apply Publisher's normal text and background formatting to any or all of the table's 'cells' (the individual compartments that contain text), so you can make the table both practical and decorative.

Tables are useful for presenting complex data on a spreadsheet, and Publisher allows you to import data that was originally set up using a spreadsheet from a program such as Excel (see page 75). But tables don't have to be limited to holding just numerical information or complicated lists. Even the simplest text list can take advantage of being arranged in tabular form by using a table frame (see Headings with information panels box, right).

Whatever the information you want to display in a table, Publisher has the tools to help you to do it. Formatting a table can make your data much easier to read, understand and use.

● **Creating a table**

If you prefer to start with a pre-formatted table layout, Publisher offers you a choice of 21 templates, suitable for different purposes, with different combinations of coloured backgrounds, rules and use of bold or italic text styles. These pre-formatted layouts are included in the Create Table dialog box that pops up when you first click the Table Frame Tool button. You can also apply one of these layouts to an existing table by using the Table AutoFormat command on the Table menu. Most of the formats have descriptive names, such as 'List with Title 1' or 'Checkbook Register', although there's a whole series simply called 'List 1', 'List 2' and so on. Fortunately, the Create Table dialog box also shows you a sample of the format and gives you a description of its

HEADINGS WITH INFORMATION PANELS

A common format for lists has a heading or name on the left and a panel of details or explanatory text to the right. Such lists can be very tricky to set up if you use tabs and indents to position the text panels. Instead, try using a two-column table. It's much simpler to lay out the list and it's easier to apply formatting. In this example, making all the names bold only required one click on the grey button above the column of names and another on the toolbar's Bold button (inset).

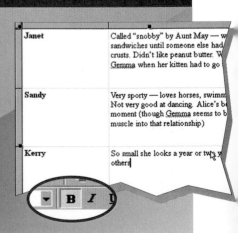

use. For example, under Checkbook Register it states: 'Use this format for presenting numbers or financial data'. There's also the option to choose a completely unformatted layout – generally the best starting point if you want a very simple, clear table or one with a customized look of its own.

The first step-by-step example (see page 74) shows how to set up a simple table using one of the preset formats and then modifies it by changing the cell sizes and the type style.

● Modifying a table

Until you start working on a table, all the other Table menu commands will be greyed out and inactive. As soon as you select an existing table (whether it was created in Publisher or imported from another program), the menu becomes active. It also becomes active as soon as you create a new table. You can then reformat the table to suit the text you want to include. On page 75, we show you how to reformat an existing table that was originally created using Microsoft Excel.

VIEWING A TABLE

While you're working on a table, the screen will display grey selection bars along the top and left of the grid (inset, below). They disappear when you move off the table, though, and they won't be printed. The same applies to the gridlines – the faint marks that separate the rows and columns on the screen. These lines are there to help you work on the table and, as with the selection bars, they will not be printed.

If you want to check how the table will look when it is printed, click on the View menu and select Hide Boundaries and Guides. If you do want gridlines to be printed, however, you can arrange for this to happen. You do this by setting their width and colour, using the Line/Border Style sub-menu, which is available on the Format menu.

Working with a Publisher table

You can produce a Publisher table using the keyboard, mouse and menus to select and edit the cells of your Publisher template chart.

TO GET TO a particular cell, you can just click on it, or you can move around by pressing the [Tab] or right-arrow keys to go to the next cell to the right, then to the first cell on the next line. Move back using the left-arrow key or [Shift] and [Tab]. The up and down arrows, as you'd expect, move up or down a row.

Selecting and formatting cells

To select several cells in a row or column, place the cursor on the cell at one end and hold down the left mouse button while you move the cursor over all the cells you want. Any formatting will apply to each of the cells you selected.

There's an easier way to select whole rows or columns. When you use the Table Frame Tool, or click on a table, you'll see thick grey selection bars at the top and the left side of the frame (inset right), divided to correspond to columns (top bar) and rows (side bar). Click in one of the divisions and you will have selected the whole row or column.

To select a number of rows and/or columns, select a corner cell, hold down the left mouse button and drag the cursor over the area you want. Any formatting will be applied to the whole area. If you want to change the formatting for the whole table in one go, just click on the button where the two grey selection bars meet at the top left. All the main selection options (rows, columns, cells, table) are also available from the Table menu.

Editing a table

The Table menu's most important editing functions are to insert or delete rows and columns. A dialog box will let you decide how many new columns or rows should be added and where they should be inserted.

If you select the Grow to Fit Text option (below), any cell in the table will expand automatically to hold the information you put into it. If you don't, any text which does not fit in the cell will not be visible (and you aren't warned about the overflow). You could change the text size to make it small enough to fit, or you could change the size of the column or row holding the cell.

You can resize the whole table by clicking and dragging the frame edge markers, but to adjust the height of a single row or the width of a column, drag its divider in the grey selection bars. Although you can change the text size yourself to make text fit, Publisher won't do this automatically when you resize rows or columns. Also, the whole table will change size by how much you enlarge or reduce a row or column. To avoid this, hold down [Shift] while resizing and the column or row next to the one you're altering changes size to take up your changes, leaving the table's overall size the same.

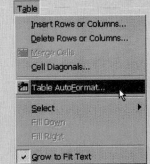

Creating a simple table

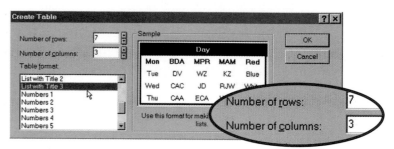

The helpers at Sandwell Lane Playgroup each do half a day during the week. Here's a form they can use for their rota.

1 Open a new blank publication. Click on the Table Frame Tool and draw a table frame filling most of the page (you'll be able to adjust the size later, so you don't have to be precise now).

2 Release the mouse button and the Create Table dialog box appears. Select a table format (we've chosen List with Title 3) and set up the table for seven rows and three columns.

3 Click OK and the table will be drawn in your document. The cursor will be waiting in the centre of the first row, which in this style is reversed out (for white text on a black background). Enter a title, choose a typeface and select a suitably large type size.

4 Now enter the rota sheet's headings: days of the week down the left in column 1, 'Morning' and 'Afternoon' in the other two columns. Select the headings and format them, setting type style and colours, using the Font Color button.

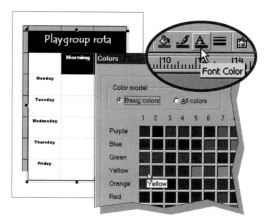

5 Now adjust the row heights. Click anywhere inside the frame to select it. Position the cursor over a row marker in the vertical bar on the left of the table; when it changes to the Adjust cursor, you can click and drag the bottom edge of that row to make the row narrower or wider. Do this to adjust the height of the top two rows.

6 Repeat the process for column widths, this time positioning the cursor on the column dividers in the horizontal bar at the head of the frame.

PC TIPS

Adding rows
The quick way to add an extra row is to press [Tab] when you're in the last cell of the existing table. A new row is added, with the cursor sitting in the first cell.

7 Now we'll add some lines between the cells. With the whole table selected, click on the Format menu and go to Line/Border Style. Select More Styles and when the Border Style dialog box appears, click on the Grid button in the Preset section at the bottom right. Select a line width. Click OK.

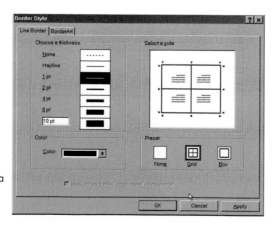

8 The table is now finished, although you might want to adjust its position on the page by moving or stretching it. Save your work and then you can print out some copies, ready to have the spaces filled in.

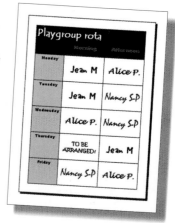

Modifying a table

We have imported a business expenditure spreadsheet created in Excel (see Importing tables box, below). Now we're going to improve its look using Publisher.

1 Start by selecting the imported table. Do this by clicking in its frame.

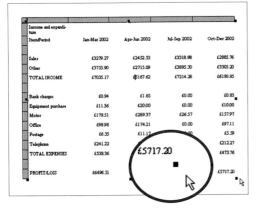

2 To apply one of the pre-formatted layouts, click on the Table menu and select Table AutoFormat. From the Table format list, choose Checkbook Register. Click the Options button and untick any of the elements of the style that you don't want – text format, alignment, patterns and shading or borders. Click OK to apply the formatting.

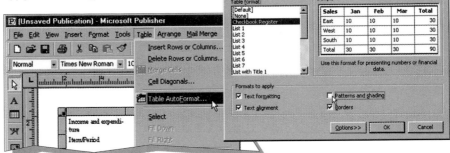

3 To tidy up the first column's width, move the cursor to the top grey selector bar and put it on the column divider. The cursor changes to a two-headed arrow. Hold down the left mouse button and drag to the right to widen the first column.

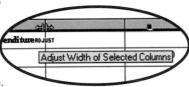

4 Go back to the selector bar and click in the second section to highlight column two. Hold down the left mouse button and sweep the cursor across the other three columns to select them. Click on the Center button.

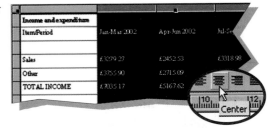

5 To make the heading more impressive, highlight the text and select a larger size and a new, bolder typeface. Make the row headings bold by selecting the first column and clicking the Bold button.

6 Now we'll stretch the heading across the whole row. Click on the vertical selector bar to select the first row – the one that contains the heading. Go to the Table menu and select Merge Cells.

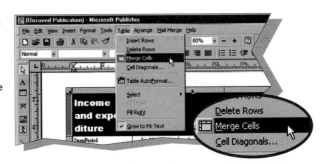

7 To highlight the totals in the bottom line, place the cursor on the lowest row divider in the grey selector bar and click to select it. Now click on the Fill Color button and choose a dramatic colour – yellow seems to work well.

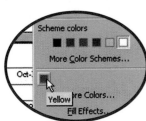

8 The table is now finished. To see how it will look when it prints, go to the View menu and click on Hide Boundaries and Guides.

Income and expenditure

Item/Period	Jan-Mar 2002	Apr-Jun 2002	Jul-Sep 2002	Oct-Dec 2002
Sales	£3279.27	£2452.53	£3318.98	£2885.76
Other	£3755.90	£2715.09	£3895.30	£3305.20
TOTAL INCOME	£7035.17	£5167.62	£7214.28	£6190.95
Bank charges	£0.94	£1.65	£0.00	£0.83
Equipment purchase	£11.36	£20.00	£0.00	£10.00
Motor	£179.51	£289.37	£26.57	£157.97
Office	£98.98	£174.21	£0.00	£97.11
Postage	£6.35	£11.17	£0.00	£5.59
Telephone	£241.22	£69.60	£354.94	£212.27
TOTAL EXPENSES	£538.36	£566.00	£381.51	£473.76

IMPORTING TABLES

If you want to edit a table created by another program, such as Word or Excel, as featured here, it's easy to bring it straight into Publisher.

Start up the program that originated the table. Select the table and copy it to the clipboard (use Edit then Copy, or hold down [Ctrl] and press [C]). Now switch to Publisher and simply paste the table straight into a document by selecting Paste from the Edit menu, or by pressing [Ctrl] and [V]. The data will appear on the page in a Publisher table frame. If its source was a Microsoft program, the table will retain all its original formats.

Adding lines and borders

Lines and borders are among the most powerful graphic tools in Publisher. You can use them to separate elements of the design, to add emphasis, or even to point to a particular spot.

Publisher allows you to draw straight lines wherever you want them. In practice, you might choose to use one as a divider between different sections or to link a caption with the picture that illustrates it. Borders are simply lines that run around a frame and can be used to make various elements of the design stand out.

Lines are created using Publisher's Line, such as Tool, while fixed borders can be added to a frame automatically. Any of the framed objects you put in a Publisher layout (photographs, clip art, text, tables and so on) can have a border that will fit the object's frame.

● Choosing a style
Lines and borders both offer many different style options. Even if you just want a simple straight line, you can set its thickness and colour. But with borders, you can also pick from a range of decorative designs, such as trailing vine leaves, many of which are in more than one colour. On the following pages, we show how you can make use of some of these items when you work on your Publisher page layouts.

To edit a line or border you use the Line/Border Style button or command.

This gives you access to all the available options, which vary depending on what you are working. When you select a line, the toolbar automatically changes to include a Line/Border Style button, which you can use to alter the size, colour and pattern of the line. There are also buttons for adding arrowheads to a line to make a pointer.

● Choosing sides
The Line/Border Style button will also appear whenever you select a frame. It gives you similar choices about the style of the lines that make up the border but you can also choose whether the border surrounds the frame or just appears on one, two or three sides. It works in the same way for text frames as for the non-text frames, such as tables, WordArt, picture and clip art frames (see pages 66-69). Line/Border Style options can also be applied to the three shapes available on the Objects toolbar: ovals, rectangles and custom shapes.

PC TIPS

If you can't see the Line/Border Style button, or if the command is greyed out on the Format menu, it means you don't have an object selected. Click on a frame or line, and the option should become available again. You can also right-click on the object and select the Change option; you'll find that Line/Border Style is one of the commands that pops up.

With just text and images, a layout can look uninteresting and unfinished. Adding lines and borders, and then choosing appropriate styles for them, can dramatically enhance your page designs.

Microsoft® Publisher

DEFAULT BORDER

You can easily set up any border pattern as the default border style. To set the default style, start with nothing selected. Click the frame or shape tool you want. Click on the Line/Border Style button, and select More Styles, then choose the options you want (including size, position and colour). Click OK to save your choice as the default. Thereafter, you'll get that style whenever you draw that type of frame.

● **Decorative border styles**

The basic border options offered by the Line/Border Style button are fairly plain. If you want something fancier, you can check out the Clip Gallery, where you will find several ready-to-go borders and frames for edges, corners and all four sides of an object. You can place these around the object and resize them, as you would with any piece of clip art.

You can also use the choices available under the BorderArt tab of the Border Styles dialog box, where there is a wide range of decorative line options, sizes and colours. You can even create a new BorderArt design of your own.

To do so, use a graphic – a clip art from the Clip Gallery or other sources, an image created with a drawing program, such as Microsoft Paint or Paint Shop Pro, or even a scanned-in image. Once you have been through the procedure, your new border will be added to the list of BorderArt on offer.

The only limitation is that if you are using BorderArt on a frame or rectangle, you will find that it usually appears on all four sides of a frame. So, if you only want a border around part of the frame, you will have to use the line-drawing tool to position the border lines where you want them.

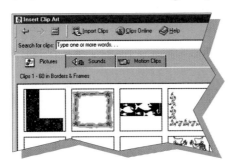
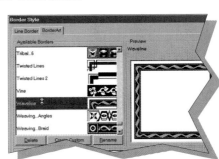

The Clip Gallery (left) contains a selection of Borders & Frames that you size and position like any other clip art objects. But BorderArt styles (right) can be applied automatically to any line or border.

Editing line styles

After drawing a simple line on your page, it's quite easy to change its thickness and colour, or even add an arrowhead, so it can be used as a pointer or direction indicator.

1 To draw a line, click on the Line Tool, position the cursor at the start of the line, and hold down the left mouse button while you drag the line.

2 With a line selected, toolbar buttons will appear, including arrow direction options and a Line/Border Style button. Use these to change the basic line shape. You can also select Line/Border Style from the Format menu.

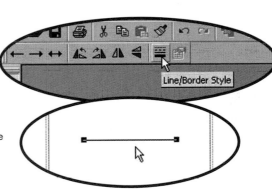

3 The Line/Border Style button only gives you basic options, so select More Styles at the bottom of the pull-down menu.

4 This gives you access to the detailed Line dialog box (right) and allows you to change the thickness and colour of the line, and add arrowheads (below).

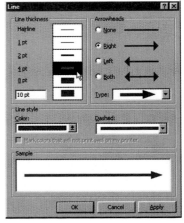
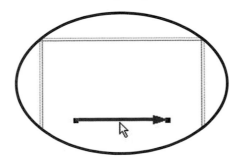

Adding a border to a frame

Putting a plain border around a frame is a simple task. Here we take it a stage further, by adding a border to just two sides of a text frame.

1 Open a new blank document. Click on the Text Frame Tool and draw a text box in the centre of the page.

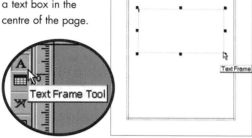

2 With the text frame still selected, click the Line/Border Style button. Select More Styles from the pull-down menu.

MORE STYLES OPTIONS

The options available when you click More Styles from the Line/ Border Style menu will vary according to the object you're working with:

● You can select line thickness and colour for all types of object.

● For all objects (except custom shapes, lines and ovals), you can specify which sides will have a border (the default is a border on all four sides).

● Arrowhead style and direction options only apply to lines; they do not apply to borders.

● BorderArt is available for all objects except custom shapes, line drawings and ovals.

3 This brings up the Border Style dialog box (see More styles options box, above right). The default border, shown in the preview image on the right, appears on all four sides. Click None (inset) to remove the existing border.

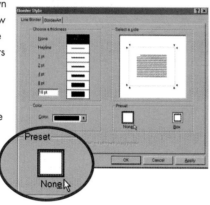

4 Now click in the middle of the top edge of the preview frame, which is headed Select a side. The marker arrows around the frame will disappear, with the exception of the two that indicate the top edge.

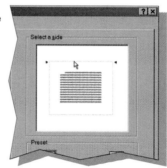

5 Hold down the [Shift] key and click in the centre of the bottom edge of the preview frame. Two more markers will appear, indicating the bottom edge.

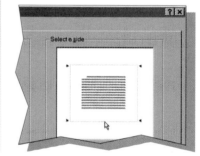

6 Select the thickness of your border by clicking one of the options. The preview should immediately show that you have created a line above and below the frame.

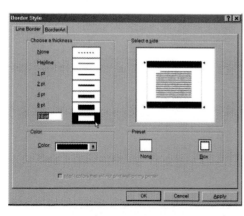

7 Click on Color and select a colour for the lines using the pull-down list. Once again, your selected colour will appear in the preview.

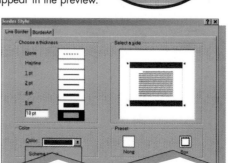

RGB(165, 0, 33)

8 Click OK and you will see your border displayed in the work area, with prominent coloured lines at the top and bottom of the frame.

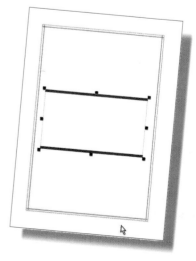

Adding a border to an object group

Here we show you how to use a styled border to tidy up the page and unify several elements by enclosing them.

1 Here we've opened a blank document and used the frame tools and the Insert menu to place various objects (including text and pictures) on the page.

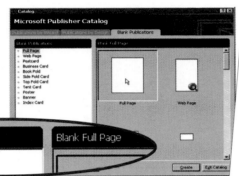

Custom shapes

Apply a border style to any of Publisher's custom shapes and the border will follow the shape's outline. But you can only use BorderArt around a rectangular outline. To put a border around a custom shape, draw a rectangle around the custom shape, then apply the border to the rectangle.

2 We have repositioned the individual objects so that they form a closely grouped panel, changing the frame sizes and text formatting as necessary.

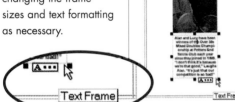

3 Now we need to draw a box that encloses all the elements. Go to the Objects toolbar at the side of the screen and click the Rectangle Tool.

4 Position the mouse pointer where you want the top left corner of the border to be. Hold down the mouse button and then drag diagonally down and to the right, until the box encloses all the objects. Release the button to complete the box. Adjust the position of each side of the new frame, if necessary.

5 On the Formatting toolbar, click on the Line/Border Style button and select the More Styles option.

BORDERS AROUND TABLES

You can draw a border around a table created within a table frame by using the Line/Border Style menu. But there is also a special method to use if you want to put lines or borders around individual cells or groups of cells inside the table. Select a group of cells, click the right mouse button to call up the Change Table menu, and then the Line/Border Style command. Click on More Styles. You'll find that one of the special options is labelled Grid; this puts the border of your specification around all of the selected cells. Alternatively, you can select a border with fewer than four sides, to be drawn around the outside of the selected cells, with no grid inside.

6 When the Border Style dialog box appears, choose the options you want for line width and colour (inset). Here, we've added a thick dark red border. Click on OK when you are happy with the preview.

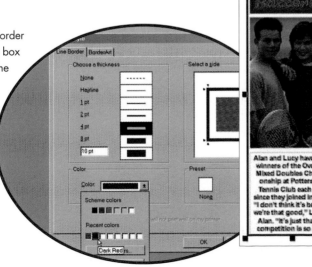

Using text styles

Text styles are a convenient way to alter typefaces, type size and other characteristics. Instead of changing each type setting by hand, program a whole set and then apply them all at once.

It's easy to change the look of any text in Publisher. All you have to do is highlight the characters and then use the Format menu to select a typeface, change its size or colour, put more space above or below the paragraph, and so on.

While this is fine for one-off jobs, many types of document have several pieces of text with the same formatting. In a booklet or newsletter, for example, it's common for all headings to share a style, for all photo captions to have the same setup, and so on.

● **Setting standard formats**
In a long document, it can soon become extremely tedious to change the style of each piece of text individually. Fortunately, Publisher offers an easy alternative: the Text Style facility. To use this, all you have to do is pre-define what a heading, for example, should look like and then save its formatting characteristics under an appropriate name, such as 'Heading'.

This style will now be added to Publisher's list of text style names. To apply the new heading style to any text, all you need to do is click on the text, select 'Heading' from the drop-down list of style names, and all the formatting instructions will be applied

instantly. The styles will apply to the whole paragraph selected – that is, all the text until the next return character – so your heading, for example, must be separated from any other text by a return. However, you can apply attributes, such as underlining, to just one word or a few words within the paragraph, anywhere you choose.

● **Why use styles?**
Apart from saving you effort, the first advantage of using styles is that it ensures exactly the same formatting will be applied every time, so all your headings, captions and so on are guaranteed to look the same. This is handy for creating a coherent look across a long or important document.

You can also import styles from other Publisher documents. This means that it is easy to create a consistent look across several different publications – so a heading can look the same in a newsletter, a report, a brochure and even a phone list.

You can reformat all text that uses a particular style simply by redefining that style. Suppose your picture caption style has the text flush left (touching the left of the frame). If you decide that you'd rather have captions centred under the picture frames, just change

Once you've set up the text styles for a Publisher document, all you have to do is apply them to the text. This overcomes the need to specify the style each time you want it changed.

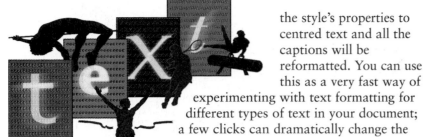

the style's properties to centred text and all the captions will be reformatted. You can use this as a very fast way of experimenting with text formatting for different types of text in your document; a few clicks can dramatically change the whole look of your publications.

● Creating and editing a style

The Text Style option appears on the Format menu. Select it when you want to create a new style, change a style or import styles from another document. You can also change a style's name here – or delete it completely.

Every Publisher document has one pre-defined style called Normal. By default, this formats text as 10pt Times New Roman, flush left, which is what you will see if you don't change the default. You can, however, alter the Normal style by selecting it in the Text Style dialog box (shown overleaf), and then clicking Change this style. Any changes you make will reformat all text in the current document that hasn't already been set to

another style or changed by hand. Other text styles can come from a variety of sources. You can define your own styles for a particular Publisher document, as shown on the next page. You can also import the styles from another Publisher document for use in the current publication (this could be a blank document that you've created specifically to hold a collection of styles), as shown on page 83. You can even import styles that have been created in other documents, such as those set up using Microsoft Word or Excel.

If you import a style with the same name as an existing style in your document, Publisher gives you a choice of overwriting the present style or bypassing the changes. The exception is Normal style, which you can't change by importing a different set of formatting characteristics from another document.

Text styles are stored within individual publications. Alterations in one publication will not affect a style with the same name in another publication, even if the style was originally imported from one to the other. To update a style in another publication, you should import it again with the changes.

Microsoft®Publisher

What's in a text style?

A style can contain any of the formatting in the first five items on the Format menu. This means a lot of settings can be applied at a single click.

HERE IS A summary of the characteristics that might appear in a text style. You don't need to set all of them, of course – those you don't modify will simply remain at the default setting:

● **Character size and type** – you can set the font, attributes such as bold and/or italic, all the special effects, such as shadowing, and your choice of underlining options.
● **Indents** – you can specify how much to indent and which lines should be indented. Conventionally, you would indent the first line of a paragraph. To emphasize quotations and other extracts, you might indent the whole paragraph on both sides.
● **Alignment** – the Indents section also lets you select a left or right alignment, or set text to be centred or 'justified' (where each full line of text is spaced out to exactly the same width).
● **Lists** – again in the Indents section, you can set up lists with bullet points (such as those that appear before the headings here), or numbering in front of each list item. You can also select alternative formats for both bullets and numbers.
● **Line spacing** – this lets you select the amount of space between individual lines, or before and after paragraphs. You can also specify spacing for characters: whether the characters should be wider than normal, whether the space between characters should be contracted or expanded, and so on.
● **Tabs** – you can choose the type of tab (left, right, decimal), its position, and what 'leader' character, such as a row of dots, should fill in the gap to the next tab.

Different documents will need different styles, and each user will have individual preferences. Here are some typical styles worth setting up, which will appear ready for use in the drop-down text styles menu (inset):

● **Body text** – used for the main text in a document. (You might want this to be different from the Normal style.)
● **Caption** – a style used for text under a photo or diagram that looks different from the main body text.
● **Contents panel** – here the main requirement will probably be tabbing, with a right-aligned tab set so that page numbers appear at the far right of the line.
● **Headings** – different 'levels' of heading for Main Headings, Subheadings, Crossheads (smaller headings that provide a visual or logical break in what would otherwise be a mass of text), and so on.
● **Lists** – it's surprising how often you need to include a list of bulleted items.
● **Normal** – you cannot remove this setting, so choose whether to leave it as the default or to modify it to a style that you will find more useful.

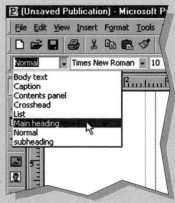

Creating a new style

**To set up a new text style, you first need a document on the screen.
Open the publication that you want to work with or a new blank
document, as we have done here.**

1 Start by clicking on Text Style in the Format menu.

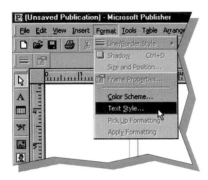

2 When you have done this, the Text Style dialog box appears. Now move to the Click to panel and click on the button next to the Create a new style option.

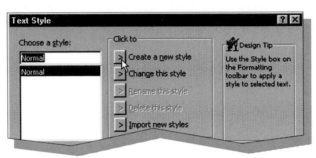

3 Enter a name for the new style you'll be producing (here we are setting up a Main heading), then move down and click the button next to Character type and size.

4 When the Font dialog box appears, make the type selections for your new style. The Sample preview panel will show you what the finished article will look like (inset). Click OK.

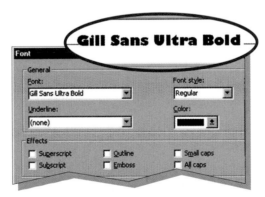

5 Go to the next item – Indents and lists – on the Click to change list (see Step 3) and click on the button next to it. Make your choices and click OK.

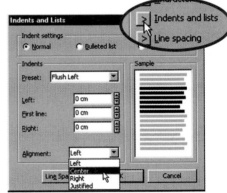

6 Repeat the process for the next item on the Click to change list and select the line spacing to be used with the new style. Again, the Sample box will show the effect of your selections. Click OK, then OK again to return to the Text Style dialog box.

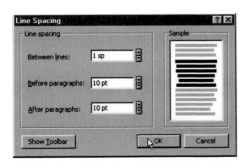

7 Repeat Steps 2-6 for as many new styles as you want (in this example we have produced four new styles in addition to Normal). When you've finished, click OK to return to the work area.

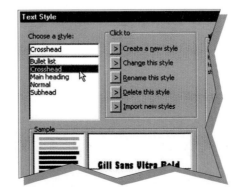

8 Save your work now and the style presets will be saved with the document. You can use this document in the exercise opposite.

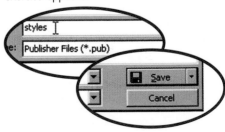

Applying styles to a document

The styles you've created can be used in an existing document which we show here using a Microsoft Publisher ready-to-go template from the Catalog.

Microsoft®Publisher

1 Click on File, then New to open the Catalog. Select the Newsletters Wizard.

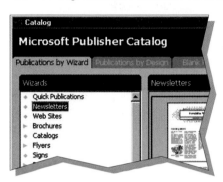

2 When you have finished setting up the document with the Wizard, click on Format and then on Text Style. When the Text Style window appears, click the Import new styles button.

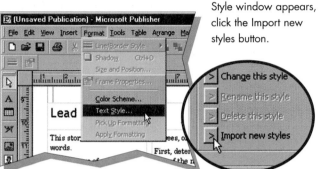

3 The Import Styles dialog box will pop up. Locate the document containing the styles that you want to include in the current publication (we've used the one saved opposite) and click OK. When Publisher returns to the Text Style dialog box, you'll see the new styles included.

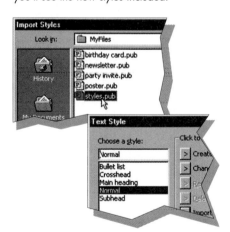

4 Click on the existing story text once to select all of it, and then press the [Delete] key. Now type in your own text to replace the deleted text. You can also insert a text file if you have already typed the text into a Word document (see Stage 6, pages 86-89).

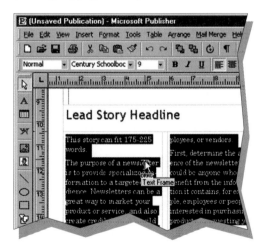

5 To apply a style, highlight the appropriate text, then click on the style names list at the far left of the formatting toolbar. Move the cursor down the drop-down list until you locate the style name you want. Click on that and the highlighted text will change.

6 Repeat Step 5 for any other text you want restyled. A new style will remain in force even if you alter the text. The style name subhead (inset) is for a secondary heading.

7 The Bullet list style is for a list of items with bullet points at the start of each item.

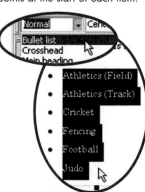

8 Save the finished document and the styles will be saved with it.

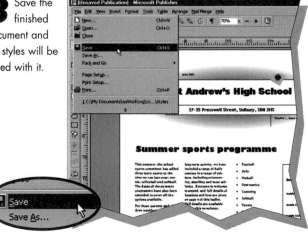

Line and character spacing

Whatever size you make the type in a Publisher document, you can change the appearance of a page greatly by adjusting the spacing between lines or individual characters – making the text look either dense or open.

When adjusting text spacing, the most important changes to make are to the space between lines and the space above and below paragraphs. These spaces are set with the Line Spacing command on the Format menu.

You can enter your instructions in several ways. First, you can tell Publisher to set the line spacing in multiples of an ordinary line. Entering a line spacing of 2 means double-spacing, and 1.25 gives you 25 per cent extra space between the lines. But you can also set a specific measurement between lines. You can enter this in inches, centimetres, points or picas. Points and picas are traditional typographic measures – a point is $1/72$ of an inch, a pica is $1/8$ inch.

If you highlight a block of text that includes more than one paragraph, the line spacing changes will apply to all the highlighted text. Otherwise they apply only to the paragraph in which the cursor is currently sitting.

● Spacing out characters

You can also change the amount of space between individual characters in text you have selected. Publisher provides two ways to do this called kerning and tracking.

Kerning means altering the spacing between given letter pairs to improve their appearance. For example, WATER looks better when the first three letters are more closely spaced than with normal spacing: WATER. Publisher kerns such letter pairs automatically (see Kerning box, right).

You're likely to make much more use of tracking (sometimes called letter spacing), which alters the space between all the

The look and legibility of a publication can be radically altered by changing the spaces between letters, lines and paragraphs.

characters you have selected. This is useful for tweaking the text to get it to fit a space. If a paragraph is a word or two too long, for example, you can tighten the space between characters to make the text fit into a frame.

You can use tracking in a more exaggerated way for headlines. Squashing up the letters can look urgent and dramatic; leaving lots of space between them can look airy and sophisticated. Many professional designers increase the tracking for text that is all in capitals. They also increase tracking for smaller type sizes and decrease it for larger ones but this is usually just a matter of personal judgement.

There are five preset options for tracking in Publisher. They range from Very Tight, which takes 75 per cent of the original space, to Very Loose, which takes 125 per cent of the original space. There is also the option to set your own values for the tracking. The range you can choose from is between 0.1 and 600 per cent. Opposite, we'll see what all this means in practice.

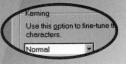

Designing with spaces

We're going to use some line and character spacing to make this restaurant menu more readable and stylish.

1 Here's a restaurant menu that has already been created in Publisher. The items and prices on the menu are in a two-column table. Click inside the table, then go to the Table menu. Find Select and click on Table to select the whole table.

2 Now go to the Format menu and click on Line Spacing. Change the Before paragraphs setting to read 10pt. Click OK. This will put more of a gap (10 points) between the items.

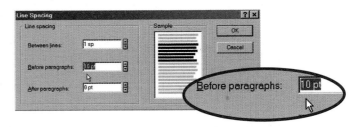

PC TIPS

The Scaling option in the Character Spacing dialog box can also change the space that letters take up. Whereas tracking and kerning affect the space

Normal text (100% scaling)
150% scaled text

between letters, scaling stretches or squeezes the letters themselves. You can use it to great effect when creating single headlines and logos, but it can make normal text hard to read.

3 If we look down the menu, we see that the last item should be one word shorter to make the table fit better on the page. Rather than rewrite it, let's try to squeeze the extra word in. Select the whole paragraph by moving the cursor over the text with the left mouse button held down.

4 Click on the Format menu and select Character Spacing. In the Tracking section of the window, change By this amount to read 98%. Click OK. This slight reduction takes the word back, but if you find that your own example needs more tracking, try a smaller percentage value.

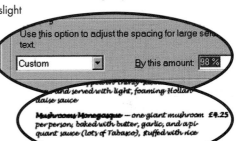

5 Now we'll put some drama into the headline. Select the word 'Menu' by dragging the cursor across it while you hold down the left mouse button. Go to the Format menu, select Character Spacing, and enter 450% in the By this amount box in the Tracking section. Click OK. This spreads the whole word across the frame – you might need to try different percentages, depending on the typeface you are using.

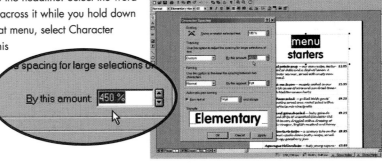

6 Repeat the process for the second word. Select the word and go to the Format menu. Click on Character Spacing. This time enter 240%. Again, you may need to experiment with the figures if you are using a different typeface.

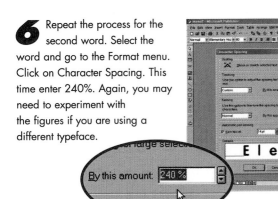

7 The result of our work is a clearer menu layout with a stylish heading.

Drawing in Publisher

If you want to include a simple diagram or chart in your publication, use Publisher's drawing tools to save yourself the bother of having to create it using a graphics program and import it into your publication.

Most of the time you'll want to illustrate your publications using clip art, photographs and other pre-drawn graphics. Occasionally, you might want to include a drawing or a diagram that you have to produce yourself.

You could easily do a job like this by using a proper graphics program such as Paint Shop Pro or even the Paint package that comes with Windows. In such cases, you have to produce the drawing in the other program, save it and then import the file into your Publisher document.

However, for simple work such as charts, sketch-maps, flow diagrams and even basic logos, you can use Publisher. The Publisher program includes its own toolkit for drawing basic objects such as rectangles and squares, circles and ovals and straight lines. There's also a useful collection of pre-drawn Custom Shapes, such as starbursts, block arrows and speech bubbles. All of these can be moved around your document, resized and coloured as you wish.

● Creating more elaborate drawings

There's also a built-in drawing facility called Microsoft Draw, which lets you achieve a lot more. Draw works in much the same way as Publisher's tools, but when you've selected the New Drawing option an extra toolbar will appear at the foot of the screen containing the Draw commands. This offers a lot more than the basic controls in Publisher. We'll be covering Microsoft Draw and its AutoShapes in more detail on pages 88-89.

Publisher's in-built facilities allow you to draw straight lines, but not curved ones. The nearest you can get to making curved lines is to use a lot of short straight lines, one after

While the options they provide are not quite on a par with those of a full graphics program, you can create some very handy illustrations using the drawing tools that come as part of the Publisher program.

the other. You can create closed curved objects, however, using the Ellipses Tool, which can draw not only ellipses but circles as well. You can also make squares, rectangles and callout boxes, which are like speech bubbles. These callout boxes can point to parts of the drawing and contain text to describe what they indicate. Callout boxes can be made to butt up to the nearest drawing object. Other facilities in Publisher's clutch of drawing tools let you rotate frames containing drawings, and add text boxes to them for labelling parts of your artwork.

Opposite, we'll see how to use some of these facilities, and we'll create a simple diagram entirely within a Publisher document.

We'll be covering Microsoft Draw and its AutoShapes in more detail on pages 88-89.

PC TIPS

Graphics

Avoid using Microsoft Draw for simple graphics, such as lines or boxes. They take up more storage space than those made using Publisher's own drawing tools, so your publication will be a smaller file if you don't use Draw.

Drawing a street map

A simple diagram, such as a sketch-map showing how to get to a party, is an ideal job for Publisher's drawing tools.

1 Open a new, blank publication. Use the Text Tool to create a heading in a large, strong typeface.

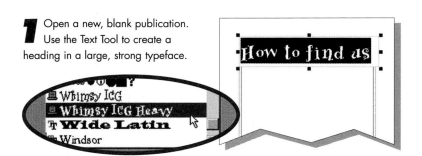

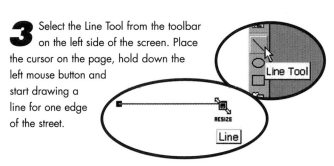

2 Now go to the Tools menu and click on Snap to Objects. With this selection ticked, anything you draw now will butt up exactly to the nearest object on the page – so you won't have to be too precise when drawing lines to make sure they meet.

3 Select the Line Tool from the toolbar on the left side of the screen. Place the cursor on the page, hold down the left mouse button and start drawing a line for one edge of the street.

4 Repeat the line drawing process until you have your street plan. Don't forget that you can always delete an error line, by selecting it and pressing the [Del] key. You can also move lines and change their length until you're happy. Now click on the Custom Shapes Tool and select the callout shape – a box with a pointer attached (inset).

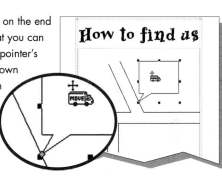

5 Click anywhere on the page to insert the callout shape.

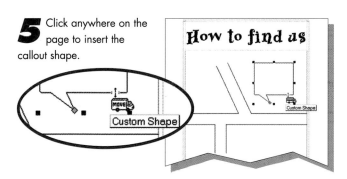

6 The grey marker square on the end of the pointer means that you can move it around to change the pointer's direction. Click on this, hold down the left mouse button, and then drag it to the right so that it now points at the road. Release the button and the callout shape is now in place.

PC TIPS

Accurate angles

You can draw a line at any angle by moving the mouse in that direction as you draw. If you want a line that's vertical, horizontal or angled at 45°, hold down the [Shift] key as you draw. The line will lock to the nearest of these three angles to the direction in which you move the mouse.

7 To add a message, click on the Text Frame Tool, draw a text box on top of the callout shape and type in your directions.

8 Click the View menu and select Hide Boundaries and Guides to see what the printed version will look like. You could add more detail with text boxes for road names, rectangles for prominent buildings, the arrows from the Custom Shapes toolkit for directions and so forth.

Advanced drawing

To create better-looking illustrations and diagrams in your publications, you can use Microsoft Draw to place a drawing area directly in your publication.

The power of Desktop publishing lies in the ease with which it lets you create attractive compound documents – publications that combine text you've typed into a word processor with tables from a spreadsheet and images created with a graphics program. However, you don't have to use other programs at all. Just as you can type text directly into Publisher's text or table frames, so you can also draw diagrams and illustrations directly in your publication.

If all you need to illustrate your document is a simple line drawing, you may find that the simple line and AutoShapes commands available from Publisher's toolbox are perfect (see pages 86-87). However, there's only so much you can do with these tools, and if you want a more colourful or more complex image in your publication, you should use the Microsoft Draw program. This works directly in your publication.

Once your picture is produced, it becomes part of the publication and the drawing tools disappear. You can resize and reposition the picture frame as usual (see pages 70-71). When you want to edit the picture, double-click on it and the Draw tools will appear.

● **Tweaking an existing picture**
You can sometimes use Draw to edit a picture that has been produced by another program. To do this, import the picture into Publisher, open up a Draw frame and use Cut and Paste to copy the image into the frame. You can then edit it. But be warned: Draw can cope with files with names ending in .DRW, .WMF or .CDR, but you might encounter problems with file names ending in .BMP, .JPG, .TIF or .PCX.

Publisher provides a clever set of drawing tools for making sophisticated images.

WHAT YOU GET

The tools provided with Microsoft Draw are surprisingly extensive. You can use them to:
● group and ungroup elements of the drawing
● align objects
● nudge objects in different directions
● turn on an invisible grid to help in aligning objects on the page
● rotate and flip objects
● include predrawn AutoShapes
● draw rectangles, ovals and lines (with or without arrows)
● include text and word art boxes
● select the colours for fills, lines and text
● select styles for lines and arrowheads
● apply shadows and 3D effects to shapes

PC TIPS

The Drawing toolbar usually appears across the bottom of the Publisher window (see opposite), but place it closer to your drawing area to minimize mouse movements as you draw. To do this drag the vertical bar at the far left of the Drawing toolbar into the document area, and the toolbar changes into a floating toolbar.

Creating a graphic in Publisher

Here we design a colourful steam engine logo for a playgroup.

1 Open a new blank publication by clicking on File, then New. When the Catalog appears, go to the Blank Publications tab and select Full Page. Click Create.

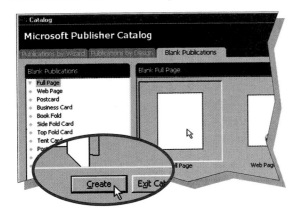

2 Go to the Insert menu. Click on Picture and select New Drawing. The screen will change to show a drawing frame with the AutoShapes toolbar towards the centre of the display and a new row of drawing tools along the bottom.

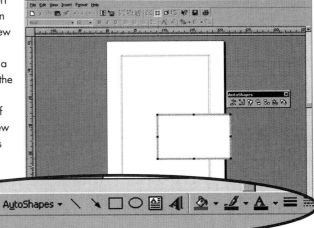

3 Don't worry about the exact position of the drawing frame for now – you can move it later. Click on the rectangle drawing tool and click inside the frame. Holding down the left mouse button, draw the body of the steam engine logo.

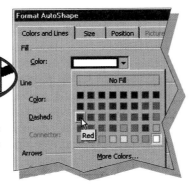

4 Finish off the engine by using other shapes from the drawing toolbar, overlaying them as required. Don't worry about the overlaid lines – we'll get rid of them later. One of the AutoShapes is a 'callout', a speech bubble described as a Cloud Callout; we can use several of these for puffs of smoke.

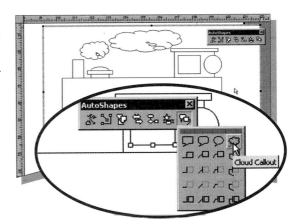

5 Now select the rectangle making up the main body of the train and click on it with the right mouse button. Select Format AutoShape from the menu that pops up. In the Format AutoShape window, go to the Fill section and click on the down arrow next to the colour bar. Click on a colour.

6 Move to the Line section and click on the down arrow next to the colour bar. Select No Line and click OK. This removes the border and fills the shape with the colour you've chosen.

7 Repeat Steps 5 and 6 for the other shapes in your drawing, adding lively colours to all of them.

8 Click outside the drawing frame to deselect Draw mode. Click once on the drawing to select it and then resize it as required before moving it to its final position on the page. Add any extra information and save your work.

Southwood Park Playgroup

Information for parents

Hardware

Slim screens

PC monitors take up a lot of desk space and also use up a fair amount of power. But there is an increasingly affordable alternative – the LCD monitor.

Nearly all home and office desktop PCs are supplied with monitors that use traditional CRT (Cathode Ray Tube) technology, which is much the same system that is used in a TV set. Because the technology has been in use for a long time, it is not only extremely effective but is also relatively cheap: you can have a large screen display of 17 or 19 inches and a crystal clear picture for only £175-£300.

● **Bulky object**
Like a TV set, your desktop monitor is a very bulky object; its 'footprint' – the area of desk space it occupies – is annoyingly large. Furthermore, it's pretty heavy and hence somewhat awkward to move to a new location. It also consumes a considerable amount of power.

There is, however, an attractive alternative to traditional monitors. LCD (Liquid Crystal Display) technology has been around since

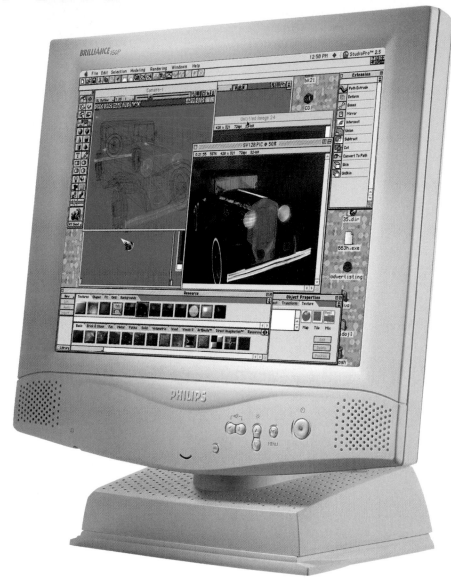

This compact Philips flat panel screen (above) is equivalent to a 17-inch CRT monitor.

the 1970s, but it is only recently that it has become a relatively affordable, mass-market, proposition.

● **How they work**
LCDs were first used in small electronic devices, such as digital watches and calculators. They work by utilizing two sheets of polarizing material, with a liquid crystal solution between them. An electric current is passed through the liquid, causing the crystals to align so that light cannot pass through them. The crystals

essentially work like a shutter: either allowing light to pass through or blocking it out. In digital terms, this gives LCDs two states: on and off, or 0 and 1. This made the first LCDs ideal for displaying a limited number of images, such as numbers on a digital watch or calculator. While this sort of simple display is very cheap, LCDs capable of displaying an infinite range of moving characters are, inevitably, much more expensive and technically more difficult to create. Until 1997, such monitors were never seen outside the more expensive laptop computers. However, today, many manufacturers offer CRT-sized

LCD monitors and this technology will certainly replace CRT completely in the near future.

● Modem LCDs

Modern colour LCDs are available in two forms, one expensive and one less so. Dual-Scan Twisted Nematic (DSTN) is a type of passive-matrix technology that uses two display layers to counteract the colour shifting that occurs with earlier LCD technology.

Passive-matrix displays use a grid of horizontal and vertical wires to define the position of each LCD element – ensuring the position of every pixel point. The quality is still not perfect, and certainly not as good as top-quality CRTs, but it is relatively cheap and is used in most budget to medium-priced portable devices.

The higher price and better quality alternative to DSTN is Thin Film Transistor (TFT) technology. This works along the same lines as DSTN, but uses a transistor to control the position and state of each pixel. This technology is known as an active-matrix display since the transistors play an active role, producing a brighter image. TFT is more expensive but is increasingly used in desktop LCD monitors.

The expense of a flat monitor can be more than justified by the saving in space it provides.

● Backlight

As well as the technology needed to create the basic image, LCDs require additional features to make them truly useful. First, a backlit display is needed to ensure a constant source of light, so enabling the foreground images, particularly text, to appear sharper in contrast to the background. Backlighting is an additional expense that some handheld devices try to do without, which is why some LCDs are difficult to read in poor lighting. As well as backlighting, LCDs also require specially created hardware to enable them to work with normal desktop PCs, although the need for special video cards is being phased out: now nearly all desktop LCDs can be plugged straight into your PC's standard video card.

Full-size LCD monitors offer substantial advantages over their CRT cousins. They are much thinner (around 6-8 inches) and so require substantially less desk space. They are also considerably lighter – a 15-inch LCD monitor weighs in at around 2.6kg. This makes a significant difference if you want to move equipment around. And they consume far less energy than a CRT monitor.

While full-size LCDs are still relatively expensive, prices are constantly being driven down as demand rises. Expect to pay around £400-£500 for a 15-inch active-matrix TFT.

● LCD pros and cons

The LCD monitor will eventually become the industry standard and the increase in use of LCDs is likely to grow gradually over the years.

Although the size, weight and performance of LCD monitors are obvious benefits, there are still significant technical drawbacks to the technology, quite apart from current pricing. The biggest problem, particularly in older LCDs, is that of a poor viewing angle. Unlike CRTs, it is difficult – though not impossible – to make an LCD monitor viewable from a full 180 degrees, which makes it hard for more than one person at a time to view the screen. Colour performance can be an issue, although this has been pretty much solved with TFT technology.

Resolution is another problem to be solved. An LCD can display only one resolution at full-screen size; lower resolutions either have to be sectioned off into a smaller part of the screen, so wasting screen space, or they have to be scaled up, often resulting in quite a serious loss of picture quality.

Notebook computers, such as Toshiba's Satellite range, depend upon colour LCD screens for their compact format and brilliant displays.

BAD PIXELS

One thing you should check before buying an LCD monitor is the company's policy on 'bad pixels'. Each pixel in a colour active-matrix LCD screen has three cells – one each for red, green and blue. Screens might often have at least one pixel which is said to be 'bad'. This bad cell might be either fixed on, so affecting the brightness, or fixed off, giving you a dark cell. If there is a large number of bad pixels, the quality of display will be poor. Manufacturers' policies on replacements vary, so do check before you buy.

Practical video editing

Whether you fancy yourself as the next Steven Spielberg or just want to get the family's home movies into better shape, it's easy to turn your computer into a powerful video editor.

As we've seen, using your Multimedia computer as a movie editor starts with getting a video capture card fitted (see pages 102-103). You'll then be able to import film sequences from a camcorder or video onto the computer's hard disk. Once that's done, you can edit your video, add titling or special effects and link up sequences to make short films.

● Capturing the video
When you use a video capture card and edit software, your computer transforms the analog video signal into digitized movie files, which you can play back on your PC. If the computer's sound card is connected to the video, you'll be able to record sound at the same time and you can add a musical soundtrack or a voice-over to the finished movie.

It is simple to make the connections between the computer and the camcorder or VCR. All you need are some inexpensive phono leads to make the basic set-up shown opposite.

● Data handling
Using a computer to work on video means processing more data than it can normally handle. Video consists of 30MB of data per second, but a typical home PC can only process one to three MB of data per second, so the solution is to use a **compression routine**. This process happens without the user being aware of it but if the automatic software compression still results in files that are too big, reducing the image size can help.

● Video editing
This is the fun part of the whole operation, although the actual process varies somewhat, depending on what video editing software you use. You might find that some software is included with the capture card, in which case try this before you buy anything else.

Be wary of splashing out a lot of money on extra editing software until you are sure you need the features it offers. However, on pages 106-107, we give an idea of just how much can be achieved with a full-featured package such as Adobe Premiere.

The principle of video editing is quite simple. Once the video footage is safely stored on your hard disk, it can be displayed much like an old-fashioned film-strip. You can move in to view it frame by frame or zoom out to view whole sequences.

A separate preview window lets you see the result of your work, while a series of tools windows gives you the editing controls.

Working with the 'film-strip', you can cut and paste sequences in a similar way to moving paragraphs around using a word processor; a running time code makes it easy to see where you are in the movie. Then you can also add special effects and 'transitions' – the various ways in which one shot can replace another. These add interest and zest to your video presentations but are so easy

that it can be hard to resist using too many effects, which distracts the viewer instead of enhancing the video.

● **Finishing touches**
Once the pictures are edited, you can add sound and text. Sound editing – whether you are adding music, speech or sound effects – works by using a visual soundtrack, which can be cut, pasted and edited in parallel with the film-strip. Sound can even be produced in stereo but, as it takes up twice the space of mono, this isn't worth using for ordinary dialogue.

SHOWING A VIDEO

An edited video can be recorded onto a blank tape in your VCR for viewing by family and friends, see below. It can also be attached to an email or even published to a global audience on a Web site.

Be aware of Internet limitations, as video files can be large and result in emails or Web pages taking many minutes to load. In extreme cases, load time can be over an hour and emails aren't delivered. Keep your clips short.

A basic home video editing set-up

With a video capture card installed, ordinary home video equipment can simply be plugged into the PC.

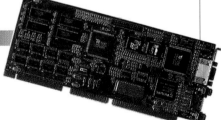

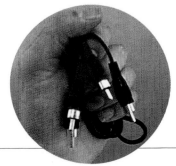

Computer
You need a fast PC with as powerful a processor as possible and lots of hard disk space.

Video editing software
(may come with card)
A video editing program will not only let you edit your tape but it will also add special effects, text, titles, sound and transitions.

Video source
Can be a video camcorder or a video cassette recorder.

Video files
Captured video is stored on the PC's hard disk. It is usually held in AVI (Video for Windows) format.

Video capture card
This goes inside your PC and converts raw video footage into a file that can be stored on your computer's hard disk. Sockets on the card's back plate provide the connections for the video cables.

Video output
Once you have finished editing your video, you'll probably want to transfer it onto a new VHS tape. You can also save it in a form suitable for using on the Internet.

Cables
All the hardware is linked by a set of cables that carry the video and sound signals. These are ordinary video cables and use phono connectors.

Video editing software

Here we take a look at Adobe Premiere, a fully featured video editing package.

It might look complex, but Premiere's main screen (below) is simple to use and includes features common to other editing packages. The largest area (in the centre) is the Construction Window, which is used for choosing and assembling clips, and there is a Preview screen (left) to see what the final output will look like.

You can click on the controls (above) to move through the video as it progresses.

You can use the Construction Window to isolate the separate clips that will make up your video. They can be displayed in the Project window (below), complete with details of their duration and size (inset).

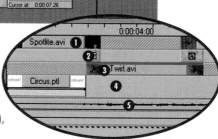

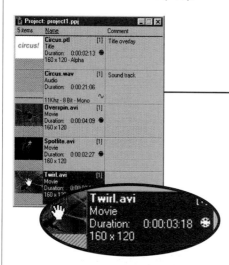

Putting together the video is a matter of choosing clips from the Project window and then dragging and dropping them into the Construction Window in the order you choose. There are five 'tracks' (right), two for video (1+3), one for sound (5), one for titles (4), and one for transitions (2).

Video editing tips

A few practical tips will make your videos more professional and enjoyable to watch.

1 Before you begin capturing and editing your video, take the time to plan it all on paper. The editing software will list each sequence and special effect, but doing the same on paper before you begin could save a lot of time later. Work out where you want each sequence to start and finish (using the time code to identify it). You might have notes saying, for example: 'Jim driving kart 00:02–00:24 – then show crash 00:56–01:16' or 'Cut out fuzzy trees 02:26–02:58'. Then list the effects, transitions, audio or text that you want to add.

2 A good home video is one which ideally maintains your interest and is entertaining. Skimp on either of these elements and people may not get much out of watching your video.

3 Take plenty of footage. The professionals always say that the most effective way to get better pictures is to take more. You can then edit them and use only the best. The rule 'Take minutes but use only seconds' is one that will keep your video scenes interesting.

4 People perceive the visual world in the following order: first we see motion, then brightness and colour and, finally, we see detail. As colour and detail are less important (especially in a short clip), we can often capture an action sequence at a low resolution to save memory.

5 Video intended for viewing only on a personal computer can save on space if you bear in mind the size that it will appear on the screen. Video made for use over the Internet is usually restricted to a smaller size (for example, 160x120 pixels) than video intended for viewing on your own computer (commonly 320x240 pixels).

Using special effects in video editing

A transition is the way one sequence swaps for another. Here we show you what two of Adobe Premiere's transitions can add to your movies.

The Transitions window (left) contains a menu of 75 transition effects, together with a description of how each one swaps image A for image B.

Making a transition

Applying a transition between one shot and another is a simple drag-and-drop affair. Pick up the transition you require from the Transitions window (top right), drag it to the Construction Window and drop it between the two video clips (right). The transition will automatically adjust itself to the correct length when placed between the two overlapping tracks.

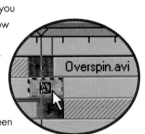

Two transitions in action

Page Peel   The impressive Page Peel transition looks as though the first shot is being picked up by one corner and then torn away (centre) like a discarded page of a notebook, to reveal the next shot underneath.

Multi-Spin   In this transition, the second image appears over the first in eight spinning rectangles (centre), which increase in size until the original image is completely replaced.

Home control

Your computer doesn't have to confine its activities to work, games and the Internet. There is special hardware and software available that allows an ordinary PC to play a major part in the day-to-day operation of your home.

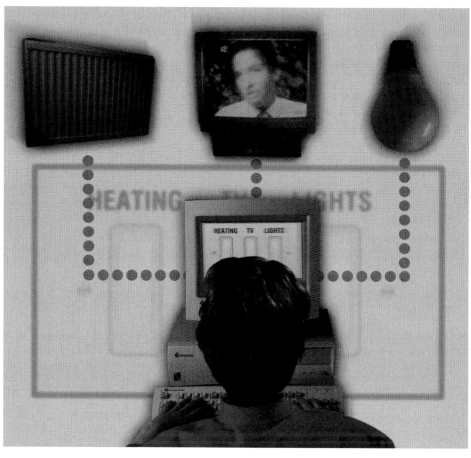

A computer and the correct software offer you many opportunities for programming your home appliances. You and your PC can be in complete control of all the electronic devices in your house.

The radio alarm wakes you up early on a cold winter morning and you notice that the bedroom is pleasantly warm, and that there is a soft light coming from your bedside lamp to brighten the gloom. You go downstairs to find that the kettle is just about to boil, ready for you to make a cup of tea. The kitchen TV has just come on, bringing you the news and weather at a suitably gentle volume. Outside, you notice the security lamps switch off as the clock ticks around to 7:30 am. The kids are just waking up to the sound of their favourite radio program, which has just clicked on in their bedroom. All is well in your automated, intelligent, computer-controlled home.

● Science fact or science fantasy?
It sounds like science fiction, but you can do all this – and much more besides – with current home automation technology controlled from the computer that's sitting on your desk right now. Astonishingly, this can all be done without rewiring your house, thanks to technology called X10, that allows you to send digital signals along the existing mains wiring to control devices throughout the house. The latest systems operate wireless technology to perform these control functions.

In the US it's estimated that over 5 million homes already have such systems installed, and similar products are now available in UK high-street electronics retailers from Martek UK, using licensed X10 technology. Software such as this gives you the power to control complicated sequences of events by entering a series of commands. These work rather like the macros you use in Microsoft Word to automate long sequences of actions (see Stage 5, pages 30-37). As the software lets you control up to 256 devices, you can run a great number of different and complex operational sequences.

● Controllers and receivers
Although X10 technology works with existing wiring, you do need some additional hardware for your

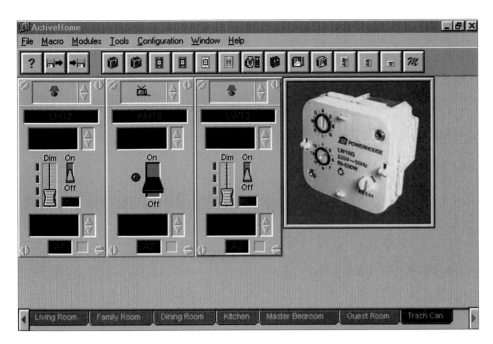

This is how the X10's software appears on your computer. You can program events to happen at certain times, or get things to happen at once by sending instructions to devices such as the one on the right of the screen above.

computer. Typically, you will need a PC interface that plugs into your computer's serial port, a universal remote control and a receiver attached to each device that you want to link to your system.

The receivers are either small plastic boxes that you plug into existing sockets, or units that replace the existing sockets. Plug in the controller, install the software and connect the receivers to the devices you want to control. Then program the computer software with the schedule of commands you want it to carry out. You don't actually have to leave the computer on for the instructions to be obeyed and you can easily re-program the software at any time. An alternative to getting your computer

to control appliances is to use a device called a mini-timer. This sends signals via the mains wiring to receivers that control your home.

● What is it all for?

The benefits of such a system are in three areas: security, energy management and convenience. If you're going on holiday, for example, you might program a sequence of events that switches lights, TV or stereo on and off to give a credible impression of the house being occupied.

In terms of energy management, a home automation system could clearly help in using power when it's at its cheapest; you might, for example, set the heating or washing machine to run when off-peak energy charges are offered.

When it comes to convenience, the applications are limited only by your imagination and the number of devices linked to the system. For example, you might want to program different sequences for when you get up in the morning and come home at night. In the first, you could program all the functions

we mentioned earlier, plus whatever else suits you and your family, such as switching on the immersion heater, setting alarms and starting the coffee machine. In the second sequence you might instruct the system to start the central heating or switch on lights.

● The future

The X10 technology is under constant development and it now includes a two-way capability. This means that you can phone home and check that everything is working properly, or alter the instructions. In addition, if any element, such as a light bulb, is malfunctioning, the system will be able to let you know.

In the future, voice recognition (see Stage 6, pages 116-117) will also become part of home-control systems. Through microphones connected to your PC, or even over the phone, you will be able to speak a sequence of commands for your computer to carry out: the system will recognize your voice and then carry out the complex set of commands.

There are different home-control hardware devices for different tasks, such as this lamp module. They can all be controlled by your computer to perform on/off commands when the programming dictates.

The range of products from Martek UK allows you to use your PC to operate many household appliances, whether you are at home or away.

CONTACT POINTS

Home Automation Range
Martek (UK) Ltd
Tel: 01359 253 555
Price: £230*
Additional accessories also available
*UK prices

Inside ISDN

ISDN is an international standard for transmitting computer data over normal phone lines. It's much faster than a conventional modem, and offers more features too.

ISDN stands for Integrated Services Digital Network. The key to understanding what it means is the word 'Digital'. Whereas a conventional modem (see Stage 1, pages 138-141) works by converting the computer's digital information into a sequence of sound waves and sending them down the telephone line, ISDN sends the information in its digital form.

This means that information can flow between computers directly without having to be converted twice. Information sent via a conventional modem must also be decoded from sound waves into digital data at the other end of the telephone line. As a purely digital medium, ISDN can transmit the 1s and 0s of binary information between computers without conversion.

● Speed benefits

On a practical level, ISDN has several benefits over conventional modems used with normal telephone lines. First of all, it's faster. The quickest modem at the moment has a maximum transfer rate of 56Kbps

(56,000 bits of data per second). However, that figure is a little misleading; it can only be achieved in one direction – when receiving or transmitting exclusively – otherwise the transfer rate drops to 33.6Kbps.

Noise on the line can slow conventional modems even more by interfering with the sound waves that represent the computer data, just as it can interfere with ordinary phone conversations, making it difficult to hear the other person. By contrast, ISDN manages a full-time speed of 64Kbps. In addition, as there are no sound waves with ISDN it is less susceptible to line noise, so full-speed data transmission is almost guaranteed.

● Two lines in one

ISDN also combines channels or pipes, of which there are two in Basic Rate (BR) ISDN connections for the home, into one line. Each of these channels works at 64Kbps. Since the channels can be combined or used independently, this feature raises the **bandwidth** to 128Kbps, allowing data transfer at around two to three times

the rate of a modem in typical situations. This is ideal for downloading large files from the Internet: where a 10MB file might take almost 60 minutes to download with a conventional modem, it would take under 15 minutes using an ISDN connection.

The two channels can also send and receive data simultaneously at 64Kbps each. This lets you interact with other computers at an impressive speed, which is useful for two-way data transfer, such as videoconferencing (see pages 148-149), and connecting to a remote office network.

This makes ISDN a popular option for linking far-flung corporate offices, teaching schoolchildren in remote locations (teleteaching) or getting the most out of employees or freelancers working from home (telecommuters).

WHAT IT MEANS

BANDWIDTH

This refers to the maximum data transfer rate possible through a connection between computers.

ISDN OR ADSL?

ISDN is clearly better than a 56K modem but it's nowhere near as fast as the ADSL (asynchronous digital subscriber line) technology that BT is in the process of implementing. Using clever data compression techniques, ADSL sends data down your existing copper telephone wires at speeds of 256Kbps up to 2Mbps. You pay a flat-rate monthly subscription of around £40-50 (depending on your ISP) and the connection is permanently on (if you want it to be) so you don't have to wait to connect. But don't rule out ISDN yet. Only those in major cities and within 2-3 miles (4km) of their local exchange will have access to ADSL. BT hopes to extend coverage to 75 per cent of the country by 2003. If you can't wait, ISDN is still worth considering.

● Faster connections

There are other benefits as well. As conversion between analog sound waves and digital computer data is unnecessary, there's no need for the synchronization routine required with a conventional modem-to-modem connection. Every modem user is frustrated by the time it takes for a connection to be established – even before data transfer can begin. A traditional modem can take over 30 seconds to connect with another, but ISDN links take less than a second.

It's possible to link up to eight separate devices – PCs, fax machines, telephones, or any combination of peripherals – to the same ISDN line. Each device can be given a unique telephone number – or more than one number, if necessary. What's more, two devices can actually use the line

simultaneously, so you can browse the Web and have a telephone conversation on the ISDN line at the same time.

● What no modem?

While ISDN does away with the need for a conventional modem, you still need a special device connected to your computer. This is a terminal adaptor (TA), sometimes also called an ISDN modem, and is used to connect the computer to the ISDN line. Just like a conventional modem, a TA can be an external device that connects to one of the computer's serial ports or a card that fits inside the computer.

Some TAs have analogue ports so that you can plug in a regular telephone handset, allowing you to talk over the same line. This saves you the extra expense of a special ISDN telephone handset, which can be quite pricey.

● Connecting a TA

A TA can be expensive. The Multitech I-Way, for example, costs around £160. However, the installation of such a device is easy: it should be no more complicated than installing a regular modem. All you have to do is turn off your computer, plug the TA into your serial port, restart and Windows finds the device. Have the TA manufacturer's disk, if there is one, standing by just in case. It's even easier if you opt for a TA which connects via the PC's USB socket. The DIVA from Eicon is one such device.

The ISDN line to your local telephone exchange will quite happily use old-fashioned copper wires if necessary. However, a small percentage of home users in the UK

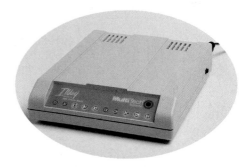

The Multitech I-Way is an zxternal ISDN modem with a built-in analogue port that allows you to connect a telephone or a fax machine.

may find that ISDN isn't available in their area due to lack of facilities inside their local telephone exchange. The British Telecom (BT) installation charge includes a 'survey' fee to determine whether or not your existing telephone line is suitable.

Once installed, you pay for what you use, and the pricing system is the same as a regular telephone line – special options and discounts apply equally to ISDN and ordinary calls. People with standard telephones can continue to call you as usual.

While costs have fallen, ISDN is still not exactly cheap. BT currently charge £49.50 to convert your existing phone line for ISDN. You then pay a monthly subscription of £40, which includes £13-worth of free calls. You will also, of course, need to buy the TA, for £100 and upwards. Finally, if you do decide to go for ISDN, don't forget to check with your Internet service provider; you will probably have to dial in to a new number to access their ISDN service.

CONTACT POINTS

British Telecom ISDN Helpline
Tel: 0800 181 514
www.homehighway.bt.com

DIVA ISDN USB
Eicon
Tel: 020 8967 8000
Price: £99*

Multitech I-Way
Multitech
Available from major mail-order and Web retailers, such as:
www.netshop.co.uk
Price: £131*   *UK prices

The DIVA from Eicon is not only small and stylish, but offers plug-and-play ISDN connectivity through your USB port – and at an affordable price.

Network file servers

Most people think of networks as the connection that links one desktop computer to another but, behind the scenes, network file servers are hard at work on everyone's behalf.

Computers that are used professionally in business and commerce are more likely to be 'nodes' in LANs (local area networks) than to be used as stand-alone machines. These LANs can range in size from only two or three machines up to several hundred PCs, plus printers and other peripherals. LANs have one special and particularly important computer at their heart – the file server.

A file server – very often a PC – is a computer dedicated to managing network resources. As the name suggests, it is the computer where files are stored centrally and then 'served' to the other PCs – known as clients –

on the network. As such, a file server is not used exclusively by any one individual on the network, but is a common, shared resource. Because of its importance in the functioning of a network, the file server has a number of distinct characteristics that tell it apart from the individual user's PC.

● **Operating system**
One area where it is different is in its software. In anything but a very small network, the file server will be running a special operating system designed for network management tasks. This software has to manage the network traffic that's constantly buzzing over the cabling. This traffic includes requests from PCs for files from the file server and may also include messages from one user on the network to another, as well as documents being sent to the printer. The speed and stability with which all of these tasks are carried out are of paramount importance.

For many years the leading network operating system (NOS) was Novell's NetWare. Microsoft then became much more involved in the supply of network operating systems. Its Windows 2000 NOS has now overtaken Novell in terms of market share. In recent years another operating system has gained a foothold in the network market. This was Linux, which some buyers saw as more stable – and cheaper – than either Novell or Microsoft products.

● **Size is everything**
The hardware make-up of file servers can vary substantially, depending largely on the size of the networks being managed and the need for reliable data access. With a very small business network – of four users, for example – an individual user's PC might act as the file server. If it has a reasonably fast processor and large hard disk, there is no reason why it

When several computers are linked together, they often have a single computer at the core of the network, called the file server. This takes care of network traffic and stores data centrally.

cannot service the limited network traffic of so few users. However, if that small business were to expand to 20–25 people, all needing to be networked, the demands on the server would require a higher hardware specification.

With this number of nodes on the network, the traffic will increase enormously. Furthermore, such a business is likely to use a 'client/ server' system. In such a system, important files, such as databases, and perhaps even applications, are held on the server and distributed to the client PCs, which return modified files to the server for storage.

● Speed

Such a small business server needs to have the right kind of hardware to handle this level of traffic. It will have a fast CPU, probably a minimum of 600MHz, and there might be the option of installing a second CPU if the computing load increases. It will have at least 128MB of RAM installed as standard, and this will be expandable up to a minimum of 1GB.

It will also have at least one fairly large hard disk (8GB minimum) already installed, with the option to add others. In order to back up large amounts of data, there is also likely to be a tape drive pre-installed. There will be plenty of expansion slots available to add further features, and there will be a network interface card (NIC) installed.

What such a file server will not have, unlike most home PCs, is either a powerful graphics card or a large monitor. These machines are for work, not play, so they tend to be supplied with only 15-inch monitors (the screen is used almost exclusively

Anonymous looking black boxes like this file server can be the heart of some small businesses.

by the network manager to monitor the status of the server and network) and none of the hardware peripherals such as joysticks.

● The enterprise server

One step up from the small business server is what the PC manufacturers have decided to call the 'enterprise server' – a bigger and faster file server designed for use in larger and more complex businesses. The needs here might include storage of and access to massive databases, and the ability to send files not just over a LAN but via links to sites in other towns, countries or continents. There will also possibly be the need for Internet commerce capability, so the hardware is upgraded accordingly. The CPU itself might be no faster than in a small business server, but instead of just one there will be the option to run as many as four CPUs together. Standard memory will be at least 256MB, expandable to as

much as 4GB. Increased data storage requirements mean that a single file server might have as many as seven large hard disks installed, giving a total storage capacity in the range of 100GB.

● Mission possible

This kind of processing and storage power implies that a business is running applications that are described as 'mission critical', meaning that if they fail, business cannot take place. With mission critical applications, security and reliability are crucial.

To cope with this, the server might well have built-in fault-tolerance features, such as 'redundant' processors, whereby if one processor fails, operations are switched to the next one. There might be a RAID system for the hard disk drives, and there will almost certainly be an uninterruptible power supply to maintain performance in the event of a power cut.

Some servers also use a technique known as 'disk mirroring', in which data is saved to two disks at the same time, so that if one fails the server switches to the other without losing data.

File servers do not necessarily cost the earth. At the bottom end, a small business server should cost no more than a powerful stand-alone PC. But as you move up the hierarchy, costs rapidly increase. For example, if you need a top-of-the-range, fully-featured enterprise server running mission-critical applications for your business, you could be looking at a price well in excess of £50,000.

WHAT IT MEANS

RAID

This stands for Redundant Array of Inexpensive Disks. It describes a system whereby two or more disks in combination provide fault-tolerant performance. The operating system thinks the drives are one single drive. If one drive should fail, the disk controller simply reconstructs the data from the other drives, and normal service is maintained without interruption.

Multiprocessing

Widely used for demanding applications, multiprocessing is a system that allows a single computer to get on with several tasks at once and so complete its work much faster.

Human beings have only one brain each, so we often enlist the help of others when we're trying to find the answer to a complex problem, working on the principle that two heads are better than one. Similarly, teamwork is a method that most companies encourage their employees to adopt.

The creators of computer hardware and operating systems have long taken this principle to heart. Modern microprocessors, such as Intel's Pentium range, and high-end operating systems, such as Windows 2000, are expressly designed to permit two or more processors to be used to deal with demanding tasks. Not surprisingly, this method of working is termed 'multiprocessing'.

● Alternative systems

There are two different types of multiprocessing. The first, known as asymmetric processing, goes back to the early days of computing. Each processor operates independently of the other and has its own memory and storage devices. They do not even need to be in the same location but can be linked by a data cable or even by a modem. This linking of separate devices is what computer terminology calls a 'loosely coupled' system.

The second type of system (the one that mainly concerns us here) is called symmetric multiprocessing – SMP. Each processor does whatever job needs to be done when it has the capacity to do it. Individual parts of a

Get a few processors working together and you can harness massive amounts of computing power.

program might be divided up between available processors. This type of operation is sometimes called parallel processing, although the term is normally used when talking about computers with a larger number of processors (see Massively parallel processing box, right).

We saw some examples of the sort of computer that uses symmetric multiprocessing when we looked at network file servers (see pages 114-115). Such computers often have to handle the network resources for a large number of users, so manufacturers offer file servers with the capacity for installing several processors. Many relatively inexpensive machines commonly include a 'dual processor' feature, while more costly servers might allow up to eight processors to be installed.

MASSIVELY PARALLEL PROCESSING

When a very large number of processors are installed in a single multiprocessing computer, the result is known as massively parallel processing. This occurs in such systems as supercomputers where, for example, an IBM computer can use 12,000 CPUs in parallel. Quite what constitutes a very large number is not clearly defined, but ten thousand undoubtedly fits the bill. By comparison, in a network file server it is rare to find more than four CPUs working together.

● Multitasking operating systems

Multiprocessing will work only if the computer is running an operating system, such as Windows 2000 or Unix, that can deal with multitasking and that is able to take advantage of the extra computing power available.

These operating systems are able to look at the available processors and decide how to assign tasks to them to achieve the best performance. Windows 2000 has the ability to assign what are known as 'threads' (a term for any parts of a program that can run independently of the other parts) to the computer's processors.

Multiprocessor systems provide the greatest benefit when a computer is required to run several tasks or to service multiple users at once. Apart from network file servers, the classic,

For computer-aided design (CAD) and graphics-intensive work such as 3D rendering, a powerful processor, such as the Octane multiprocessor from Silicon Graphics (above), is needed.

everyday application for multi-processing can also be found in a bank's cash machine network.

● Immediate response

Such applications are known as Online Transaction Processing (OLTP). This is the term for the type of job in which the computer has to respond immediately whenever a user makes a request. Multiprocessor computers are able to service many more requests than a single-processor server, and without delay – clearly important in a busy banking network handling a great many transactions.

● Extra power, extra output

Even a system used by a single, 'power' user could benefit from multiprocessing. For example, architects and engineers who use computer-aided design (CAD) programs frequently need to take a set of line drawings and render them as a solid 3D object to calculate subtle colours and shading.

This might tie up a single-processor computer for hours, stopping the user from doing anything else on the system. But with even a two-processor system, one can be left to handle the rendering while the other is free to run different applications. For many businesses, the cost of the extra processor could easily be offset by the increase in productivity.

But simply adding processors is not enough in itself to ensure significant speed improvements. Since each processor in a multiprocessing system might share resources, such as memory, disk drives and a network card, four processors will not give exactly four times the practical performance of a single one.

Designers of multiprocessing computers are, of course, well aware of this and make allowances by ensuring that the other parts of the system are as fast and efficient as possible so that they can make the most of the extra processors. This means using large amounts of cache and main memory, fast disk drives and RAID systems (see pages 114-115), so that data can flow

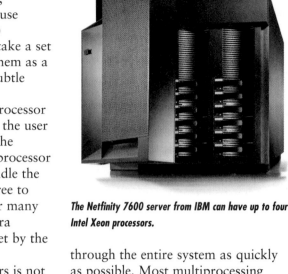

The Netfinity 7600 server from IBM can have up to four Intel Xeon processors.

through the entire system as quickly as possible. Most multiprocessing systems are also designed to be 'scalable', which means that they can be expanded as the need arises, by fitting extra processors, additional memory, disk drives and so on.

● Future implications

Multiprocessing systems were once considered important mainly for file and database servers. However, the falling price and increasing performance of multiprocessor technology means that it is now increasingly used in desktop computers that are intended for processor-intensive work, such as complex financial modelling.

Multiprocessing at the level that it is used in the workplace has yet to make inroads into home use, where the pace of a single Pentium processor will probably prove quite fast enough for some time to come.

The Compaq Proliant 8500 server multiprocessor can be fitted with up to eight Intel 700MHz chips.

RISC processors

Not all home computers use Pentium-based PCs; some have had great success by adopting processors that take a RISC.

There are many different ways to speed up the operation of a personal computer – from using faster types of memory to increasing the speed of devices such as hard disks. But over the years, computer designers have still not managed to come up with a better solution than making the microprocessor at the heart of the PC work faster.

In the 1970s and 1980s, many computer designers began to believe that extra speed could be achieved by rethinking the way in which chips were designed. They hoped to be able to get a microprocessor to carry out its job more efficiently by redesigning what, in their jargon, they called the 'architecture' of the chip.

● Keeping it simple

The chips they created became known by the acronym RISC, which stands for Reduced Instruction Set Computer. The name means that this type of microprocessor is designed to recognize only a relatively limited set of instructions – in contrast to the previous design philosophy, which depended on complex commands that, in turn, demanded the creation of ever-more complicated microprocessors to use them. A RISC system uses a large number of simple, basic instructions, which are all the

This 64-bit RISC chip from Sun Microsystems is designed to be used in an extremely powerful workstation.

Apple's stylish new G4 iMac uses a fast RISC chip made by Motorola to bring great computing power to ordinary users.

CLOCK CYCLES

Microprocessors contain many transistors (around 28 million of them in the case of the Pentium III) mounted on a sliver of silicon. Each transistor can be turned on or off. The opening and closing of these transistor 'gates' is regulated by a clock, with its speed measured in megahertz or millions of ticks per second.

This is why a computer's clock speed affects its efficiency. The faster the clock speed, the faster your computer works; a 750Mhz PC is substantially quicker than one running at 300MHz. But things will also speed up if it is possible to reduce the number of clock cycles taken to perform a single operation. The aim of RISC systems is to achieve one operation per cycle.

same size. Because each instruction is so simple, it can be processed very quickly. In effect, RISC aims to speed things up by breaking up a large problem into lots of smaller ones and solving them faster.

● Rival systems

But RISC displayed problems of its own, as we shall see later, and the older approach did not die out with its arrival. Indeed, the chips in most of today's computers still use complicated instructions – in what became known as CISC, for Complex Instruction Set Computer (a name that didn't exist until the development of RISC).

In a CISC machine, a single instruction (such as adding two numbers together) will depend on lots of complicated instructions. Nothing can happen until the previous step has taken place, so this is guaranteed to be a slow process. In a CISC system the processor might need between four and ten clock cycles (see Clock cycles box, on opposite page) to perform a single instruction. One of the fundamental goals of the RISC approach is that a single operation should be completed in only one cycle.

● Pros and cons

When they started to make their mark in the mid-1980s, RISC systems could have been expected to take over the world. They were even attractive for a reason other than just speed; the chips were considerably cheaper to manufacture.

As they contained fewer individual components, the chips could also be physically smaller and produce less heat, saving PC manufacturing costs in terms of cooling fans and power systems. But, despite offering speed and cost advantages, RISC systems are not without their drawbacks.

● Compatibility

Chief among these is that computer users want to retain compatibility with the software and operating systems they have already invested in.

PIPELINING AND SUPERSCALAR DESIGNS

Pipelining is central to the RISC idea. Instructions are broken up into smaller micro instructions, which are carried out by different parts of the processor in an 'execution unit'. Such a unit can deal with up to seven instructions at once, all at different stages of completion. The goal is to perform one instruction per clock cycle, although this is not always achieved in practice.

In superscalar designs, the RISC chips contain multiple 'execution units' that allow the processor to execute several similar instructions at the same time, thus increasing speed still further. But as modern CISC microprocessors also use pipelining and superscalar techniques to increase their speed, the absolute speed advantage of RISC has not been maintained.

Throughout the history of the PC, these have largely been written for Intel's CISC-based microprocessors.

Each new version of the Intel chips can run older PC software but this would not be the case if PC manufacturers switched to a RISC system. The Windows operating system and applications programs would then all have to be rewritten to take advantage of the different type of microprocessor. Some computer manufacturers made RISC-based PCs, and Microsoft even made a special version of Windows for it. However, it failed to take off and has largely been abandoned by both PC users and manufacturers alike. However, RISC systems have made major inroads in specialized fields, such as the graphic workstations used

Inside their mini-tower enclosures, some of the newest G4 PowerMacs from Apple now sport twin RISC chips in a multiple-processor setup.

for 3D modelling, games design and computer-aided design (CAD). Here, companies such as Hewlett-Packard and Sun, with its range of SPARC stations, use RISC processors because they offer a good trade-off between computing power and price.

One place where RISC has won many fans is in the Apple Macintosh computer. PowerMacs and iMacs all use derivatives of Motorola's Power PC RISC chip. Despite running at slower speeds than similarly priced PCs, these Macs work just as fast – thanks to the RISC benefits outlined earlier.

● The end of the contest

In some respects, the whole RISC versus CISC debate is beginning to look a little old fashioned. To increase their power, many RISC processors are now using as many instructions as some CISC processors of the recent past.

CISC chips from Intel and other manufacturers are using techniques that were once limited to RISC chips. The MMX unit in a Pentium II, for example, deals exclusively with certain operations involving graphics, sound and video, using a technique called SIMD – Single Instruction Multiple Data. This also resembles the way RISC works.

Chip designers on both sides of the CISC/RISC debate are likely to continue to adapt the best technology from the opposite side in order to keep up with the continually increasing demands placed upon chips by computer software.

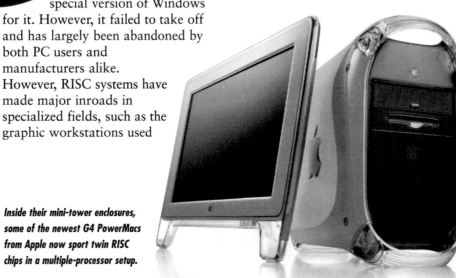

Home Learning & Leisure

Computing in shops

When you get to a shop's checkout, the chances are that the job of totting up your bill and printing out a receipt falls to a computer that's a very close relation of the PC on your desk at home.

Go into virtually any shop, whether it's a corner newsagent or a huge supermarket, and you can almost guarantee that your purchase will be logged on an electronic till. Although, with all its extra appendages, the electronic till might look like a completely different machine, it is essentially a PC, with many of the same components as the computer in your home or office. It has the same type of microprocessor, and an operating system which is likely to be a variant of MS-DOS and Windows.

● Looks aren't everything

Despite their different appearance, such till systems use familiar computer components and have familiar input and display devices: the keyboard and the monitor. But in this case the keyboard might be built into the PC itself and be fitted with a credit/debit card reader. There might also be an additional mini-monitor, which can be rotated to face the customer so that he or she can see the cost and total of the items bought. A printer, or even two, outputs receipts and this, too, might be built into the system unit. But, perhaps the most significant difference from a home system is the bar code reader.

● Instant information

Bar codes are essential to modern point of sale (POS) systems. A bar code is a printed series of parallel bars and lines, usually black on white, used to represent the binary digits that computers deal in. As such, a bar code can be read instantly by an optical scanner (the bar code reader) connected to the PC till. There's a bar code on the back cover of this book.

● Processing the data

How the till deals with this data from the bar code is central to the computing process in the retail industry. In the supermarket, the checkout operator passes your jar of coffee across the scanner and the item and price are registered. These details are added to the bill, which is totalled up and printed when your basket is empty. You offer payment (cash or a credit/debit card, whose magnetic strip is read by the computer), and you are given your receipt. The obvious benefits are speed and accuracy – there's no laborious keying in of prices, so there's less chance for the operator to make mistakes.

The amount of work that goes on behind the scenes in a busy shop is vast. Without computers to help, it would be extremely time-consuming to run such a business.